D1516022

HF
5549
.5
R58
S73
2006

# TALENT BALANCING

# TALENT BALANCING

*Staffing Your Company for Long-Term Success*

JIM STEDT

**LIBRARY**
**NSCC, WATERFRONT CAMPUS**
**80 MAWIO'MI PLACE**
**DARTMOUTH, NS B2Y 0A5 CANADA**

Westport, Connecticut
London

**Library of Congress Cataloging-in-Publication Data**

Stedt, Jim, 1948–
    Talent balancing : staffing your company for long-term success / Jim Stedt.
        p. cm.
    Includes bibliographical references and index.
    ISBN 0–275–98579–2 (alk. paper)
    1. Employees—Recruiting.   2. Personnel management.   3. Employee selection.   4. Success in business.   I. Title.
    HF5549.5.R58S73   2006
    658.3'11—dc22        2005020946

British Library Cataloguing in Publication Data is available.

Copyright © 2006 by Jim Stedt

All rights reserved. No portion of this book may be reproduced, by any process or technique, without the express written consent of the publisher.

Library of Congress Catalog Card Number: 2005020946
ISBN: 0–275–98579–2

First published in 2006

Praeger Publishers, 88 Post Road West, Westport, CT 06881
An imprint of Greenwood Publishing Group, Inc.
www.praeger.com

Printed in the United States of America

The paper used in this book complies with the Permanent Paper Standard issued by the National Information Standards Organization (Z39.48–1984).

10  9  8  7  6  5  4  3  2  1

I would like to dedicate this book to my mother, Ann Stedt, who taught me to see the good things in life and never to give up.

# Contents

# Preface

## A BRIEF ECONOMIC HISTORY

The decade of the 1990s saw the economy skyrocket. The stock market went from below 3,000 to over 16,000. The gross national product (GNP) went from $6 trillion to $9 trillion. The result was a major shortage of employees. It was difficult to find people to fill open positions, and it was often impossible to find *good quality* people. The shortage opened the door for the professional recruiters and "headhunters." They were hired as consultants, full time and part time. Companies were hiring twenty, thirty and forty people at a time, with little thought of slowing down. The country went into a hiring frenzy. Practically every organization had openings and people were job hopping so much you never knew where they were! Almost every industry was hiring; part time, full time, right out of school, right out of the military, and off shore, there were more jobs than people, and organizations had large groups of people in Human Resources (HR) dedicated only to recruiting. In addition, there were a lot individual contributors who were promoted to management positions because of the shortage. These people had no experience in evaluating resumes or interviewing people. But people were needed and there was lots of money to spend on "staffing up."

Then times started to get tougher. The dot-com industry crashed and burned, followed shortly by a recession in the high-tech arena. The stock market dropped and the ripple effect sent shudders through all industries. Job openings were frozen, layoffs started occurring, and entire departments of recruiters were dismissed. Companies dedicated only to recruiting and temporary services closed their doors. The economy went from hiring anyone to hiring no one! Even HR departments trimmed down to fighting weight. An additional problem plaguing the business world were all those inept managers who did not know how to manage in crisis mode and started driving people out of companies that stabilized.

Slowly, from 2001 to 2005, the economy has started to modestly grow again. The stock market has grown to nearly 11,000. Companies found out that they could run with fewer people but could not grow without hiring. A lot of companies are gun shy and have held off hiring because they do not want to go through layoffs again if the economy falters. The companies who were hiring twenty to forty people at a time during the 1990s are now just hiring three to five people. Now, however, they have to hire without recruiters or an HR staff that is experienced in recruiting. Companies cannot afford to hire incompetent people again. They can't hire just anybody—it is too expensive—and they have to have everyone count in order to make profits. Organizations today also are finding it difficult to hire good people because the pool of candidates is dominated by the poor performers who were the first to be laid off.

Companies must train HR staff or hiring managers who have little experience at recruiting. It may be too expensive to outsource the recruiting effort. So small HR staffs or hiring managers must recruit, even if they don't like it or know how. In the near future, it is going to get tougher out there. According to my analysis of recent Bureau of Labor Statistics information, there will be 10 million more jobs than people to fill them by 2011. In addition, they have estimated that over fifty-five percent of employees will leave their positions within twelve to eighteen months of starting. So much for stability!

The biggest challenge that all companies face today is recruiting good-quality people. A recent study found eighty-five percent of surveyed companies said "attracting and retaining the *right* talent was *very important.*"[1]

## PEOPLE WHO CAN USE TALENT BALANCING

This book has been written for anyone who must hire, manage, and retain a workforce. It will work for everyone from a new supervisor to the company president. If you want to be a supervisor, manager, or hiring manager, *talent balancing* will show you how to do it. It is not a trial-and-error method. It will work for you if you implement it properly. If you are an HR employee and have not been involved in recruiting, this book will give you the process, forms, policies, and procedures to hire good-quality people in an acceptable time frame. It is important to follow the process in the second half of the book step by step and not to jump around because each step is incremental and each builds on another. Hiring managers who have trouble with the people they employ will learn what to do to attract good-quality people. New managers will have a step-by-step process to follow that will impress even seasoned managers. New business owners and entrepreneurs will learn how to build their organization with people who share their own goals and objectives. It will also give them the twelve steps to reality management (see chapter 1), which will teach them how to retain and motivate their staff.

## COMPANIES AND INDUSTRIES THAT CAN USE
## TALENT BALANCING

It does not matter if you are a start-up, small company, or mature organization, talent balancing can and will work for you. It may take larger companies longer to implement because of the red tape and numerous meetings that have to be part of the process. But talent balancing will work; all you have to do is make it happen. Almost all industries can learn and use talent balancing techniques. It does not matter whether your company is product or service oriented, whether you sell retail or wholesale or business-to-business. This book covers the basics for all businesses.

## SO WHAT IS TALENT BALANCING?

When incompetent people are hired and placed in the wrong positions, they become engrossed in office politics and don't know, or care,

*Flaming enthusiasm, backed up by horse sense and persistence, is the quality that most frequently makes for success.*

—Dale Carnegie

about company goals. Under these circumstances, the organization will founder and eventually fail. In addition, a lot of health and other stress-induced problems will bother the workforce long into the future.

The philosophy of talent balancing is, in point of fact, fairly simple: Find the best people you can, use all their talents to meet personal and corporate challenges, and provide leadership that encourages communication, creativity, and accomplishment. It is a dynamic process that works in all industries.

As we reveal in chapter 1, establishing your corporate goals and reinforcing your corporate culture must be the foundation of talent balancing. You must have a direction and working philosophy to achieve it.

Success is a team effort. No one person can do everything alone. A secure, energetic and confident environment will create a synergy that will tap into the organization's creativity and resourcefulness. The result will be a business with a superior attitude, excellent work ethic, and a "can-do" posture.

There is magic in a team that works together for a common cause. In the United States, for example, we may fight among ourselves, but when we are attacked from outside our borders, we put our differences aside and join together as one unified, unbeatable, united force. Businesses should emulate this type of focused activity. Staff at too many companies fight among themselves as if they were enemies. They must realize that the real enemy is the competition. They forget that the best way to survive in the business jungle is to become a united team.

What ties the structure of talent balancing together is reality management (the twelve steps of which are outlined in chapter 1). Upper and middle management must know how to run a company of superstar employees. When you start using seventy-five percent of your time playing politics and twenty-five percent of your time doing your job, something is going to give. When management plays games and lies to the employees, trust and honesty disappear and the company begins to fail. Consider the following example:

---

A company had been losing money for almost a year and got to the point that they had to have a twenty percent layoff. It was a real secret until that fateful Friday. The following Monday, upper management called in all the directors, managers, and supervisors and told them that the layoffs were over and they needed their support to meet the quarterly goals with the reduced workforce. They were also told that they would back up all middle management decisions. But the following Friday, there was another layoff that again was unknown to middle management. The Monday after the second layoff middle management was brought in again and told that they inadvertently left some people off the first layoff list but now they had everybody and the current population was stable. Middle management once again went back and tried to figure out how they were going to meet the objectives with an even smaller work force. On the next Friday there was a third layoff! Upper management didn't even try to have a third meeting to explain it. Middle management was so disgusted with the incompetence and dishonesty that most of them quickly started looking for new jobs. Fourteen months later the company went bankrupt. Upper management could have saved the company if they took the key employees into their confidence. They also could have used some of middle management's experience and knowledge to help with downsizing and coming up with a recovery plan. People can be very creative when they have to be.

---

*Talent Balancing* is not a book of theories; it is based on over thirty-five years of actual business experience and real-life answers to real-life business problems. It is a process that shows you how to:

- Analyze what works (and what does not work)
- Make realistic plans for the future
- Expose the poor performers
- Recruit the good employees
- Manage them properly
- Make changes in staff and the work load to continually balance your talent
- Assist your staff in expanding their work experience
- Retain your superstars by using the twelve steps of reality management

The real magic to talent balancing is that you implement it in the order in which it is presented. You cannot put the cart before the horse. I suggest that you read the book through completely then go back and put each chapter into practice one at a time. Forms, policies, procedures, and step-by-step instructions are included. You don't even have to add batteries!

Running a business and trying to implement changes has been compared to "tuning the race car during the race." Talent balancing will give you the tools to make the major changes to your business to make it successful. Talent balancing is not complex but it does help solve complex business problems. Remember, you may have justifiable false starts and slow downs, but if you make a concerted effort to make it work, it will work!

## ON THE PERSONAL SIDE

I wrote *Talent Balancing* using over thirty-five years of actual business experience. All the case studies in this book are based on actual events that were experienced by me.

In 1969 I started gathering data and doing research for this book, although I didn't know it at the time. I was a Class III Jr. Engineer (they call them technicians today) fresh from college and just starting to learn the reality of the business world. After six months on the job, I started taking notes on how to manage people and created policies and procedures that would handle eighty percent of recurring problems. Since none of the other customer service or factory repair engineers wanted to supervise or have anything to do with the paperwork, I was assigned as a supervisor, but no one officially reported to me nor was my title changed. I analyzed workflow and determined the best way to quickly and efficiently move the repairs and refurbishments.

As the years went by, I started to create more formalized policies and procedures with forms, schematic work flow diagrams, and notes on what worked, what didn't work, and why. As management made illogical decisions, I would write down what I would do and why. I started creating a series of notebooks as my own Encyclopedia of Business Knowledge. Early in my career I was asked by a number of hiring managers to assist in the interview process, which I enjoyed. I continued to create questions for interviewing along with evaluation forms and procedures to make the process fast and well-organized. When I was working for a computer division at one of the major phone companies, I was involved with the corporate policy and procedure staff. My knowledge of corporate America grew quickly as I became involved in accounting, manufacturing, quality, sales, marketing, and human resources.

In the mid 1970s I had finally landed a management position in which I managed a staff of five, which was later expanded to thirty-five. I finally had a chance to prove my management theories. In addition, I could test the recruiting, interviewing, and hiring techniques I had developed. This gave me the opportunity to field test all my ideas, modify them as required, and update my encyclopedia of business knowledge. I was amazed that most all of the concepts worked and were well received. Two of my prime directives were to "not reinvent the wheel" and "if it works, don't fix it." The basics have not changed much over the years.

I started Hartley & Associates, my own consulting business, in 1984. By this time my personal encyclopedia of business knowledge library was up to fourteen volumes, each four inches thick. We started as a management consulting and marketing research firm. We would go into an organization, take over a department, establish the goals and objectives, create the policies and procedures, then hire and fire staff and balance the talent with the workload, and bring in a manager or director to carry out the plan. We did not realize it at the time, but we spent a lot of effort in the hiring process to get the right people in the right positions. By the early 1990s, our business had morphed into recruiting and organizational development. More and more efforts were going into helping inexperienced hiring managers staff their entire departments. We were also working with start-ups that were just establishing their own corporate culture while growing the organization and attempting to meet tight time frames.

In 1998, *MicroTimes Magazine* asked me to do a monthly "Careers" column. The senior editor decided that it would not be the typical "how-to-get–a-job" column, but would be more from the viewpoint of management, both the hiring manager and upper management. I started to get a lot of feedback from people embracing the recruiting and management techniques presented in the articles. I had struck a chord with business America. One day, while working with a new biometric company, I was trying to explain our management and hiring concepts to a vice president. I used the term *talent balancing* to explain the concept and it stuck. Talent balancing gave the vice president a unique mental image of the needs of the organization.

Since 1984, the Hartley & Associates staff has worked with over 150 companies. Every company is different, but we have seen classic business problems in almost every one. Business is difficult because it is always in a state of flux. Companies hire, then they fire, then they hire back again because they fired too many people the first time. They get caught up in a roller coaster of hiring and firing. They start changing directions and products and services. Employees get confused and are no longer loyal to the company. It is rare to see people staying for more than two years at such a company. It is harder and harder to determine what the workload is going to be and how to handle it. We are in an economy that is impossible to predict and is not reacting as other economies have in the past. Managing is more and more difficult due to all of the rapidly occurring changes. Inexperienced managers are pushing companies into bankruptcy, while creating stress and ill will on the part of the rest of the organization.

As I spoke to my peers in other industries, I realized that the basics of talent balancing cross all trades and businesses. The basics of business are always the same: getting skilled people to produce a product or service that makes a profit and creates a future for the company and its employees. It does not matter if you are selling a service or product, or are a software company, ad agency, mortgage firm, retailer, or manufacturing business; you are facing the same basic problem: "How do I hire and retain good people for long-term success?"

Good luck and good successes!

### Special Notes

- Every state has its own laws governing the employer-employee relationship. Please review the laws of your own state before proceeding into a formal staffing program.
- All the case studies in this book are based on actual events that were experienced by the author.
- While all Internet addresses are valid as of the accessed dates listed in this book, they may move or change over time.
- Talent Balancing™ and Reality Management™ are trademarks of Hartley & Associates.
- All the forms found in this book, along with chapter addendums and updated information, can be found at http://www.talentbalancing.com. Please use the password PCTSEB1 to gain access to the special download section.

### Note

1. Steve Gross, "Perspective: 2005 US Compensation Planning," September 2004. Available at: http://www.mercerhr.com/knowledge center/reportsummary.jhtml/dynamic/idContent/1156265;jsessionid CIJKKDNOCHL2MCTGOUFCIIQKMZ0QUI2C. Accessed

# Acknowledgments

Thanks to my former bosses who believed in me and gave me an opportunity: Roy McDorman, Ron Bachelor, Gary Owen, Earl French, and Al Rider.

Special thanks to my associates, friends, and colleagues who have worked with me, supported me, and laughed at all (well most) of my jokes: Mario Aldana, Joyce Arntson, George Carson, Jerry Chase, Richard Daugherty, Tom Edwards, Jim Getzinger, Richard Glass, Galen Guseman, Steve Hammett, Dr. George Hess, Bob Hosale, Stephen Lawton, Rob Moore, Rick Moss, Nick Philipson, Joan Ramstedt, Dick Ranes, Rick Rawson, Larry Slaten, Mark Stein, and John Vickers.

# CHAPTER 1
## What Is Talent Balancing?

---

### Talent Balancing

*The ability to balance the workload with the appropriate and competent staff. The objective is to be able to produce goods and services to meet corporate goals with a minimum number of employees working at the highest level of productivity. At the same time, employees need to be challenged, comfortable with their responsibilities, and capable of meeting their goals. Talent balancing is a dynamic process—it always involves a specialized methodology in recruiting staff with an eye toward balancing current and future capacity and goals. It also builds teams that stay together and continue to be very efficient and productive. Finally, talent balancing includes an effective management technique in order to keep the staff challenged and fulfilled.*

---

There is more talent in your company than you realize. Most of upper management does not know the complete background of their employees. When employees are first hired, the natural inclination is to focus on their skills for the position being filled at the time. Anyone with more than a few years of experience is unlikely to have everything they have accomplished—or are capable of doing—on a two-page resume! In order to assess the capabilities and potential of your workforce, and to incorporate the philosophy of talent balancing into your staffing,

### Job Seekers

48% of professionals are engaged in active job searches

33% of professionals are "keeping an eye out for new opportunities"

*Source:* "Poll says heavy turnover expected; both human resource professionals and employees expect heavy turnover when the job market improves, says a SHRM survey," *Work & Family Newsbrief*, October 2003. Available from http://www.findarticles.com/p/articles/mi_m0IJN/is_2003/Oct/ai_109040005#continue. Accessed September 14, 2005.

recruiting, hiring, and ongoing management strategies, you need to dig deeper than the resume. You need to know your staff through conversation. Who are the fast learners? Who is not being challenged enough? Who has other experience or expertise that is not being tapped?

When hiring new talent, it is, of course, important to determine exactly what background and skills are needed to fulfill the requirements of the open requisition and position. At the same time, however, you should consider the other talents the candidates have that may be transferable to future products, projects, and initiatives. Although it is impossible to know exactly what the company will be doing or needing in one to three years, most upper management will have a "feel" for where the company is heading. (And if they don't, they and the company are probably in trouble!) This corporate gut feeling, along with formal plans and directions, will lay the groundwork for expanding a job description into other areas where candidates may be used in the present and in the future. The talent balancing process takes the guesswork out of the planning, hiring, and managing of staff. By following this book, you will be able to start hiring capable people who will be able to get the job done and be prepared for new challenges.

Ideally, your company will always be perfectly staffed to meet current goals. It will challenge and motivate employees, operate at full capacity, and generate high profit margins—and be primed to adapt to future challenges. But in reality, at any one time, your company will be wrestling with at least one of three talent balancing challenges:

- Hiring before people are needed (The Hiring Frenzy)
- Laying off the wrong people or too many people (When Downsizing Becomes Capsizing)
- Needing to hire missing talent (No Cooks . . . Or Broth)

Your company will go through a number of life cycles from start-up, through rapid growth, to evolving into a mature organization.

Although talent balancing can be applied to any of these stages, it is better to establish it as early in the life cycle of the company as possible. By doing this, talent balancing becomes part of the corporate culture much more quickly. Mature companies have a more difficult time making changes. They, like some people, become set in their ways. Corporate management must take the lead and be responsible to drive the change process through the organization. A company will grow, shrink, and change products and/or services. People will come and go and the economic weather will continue to change. The typical twenty-first century company has many challenges and should not have to worry about losing employees to competitors or not being able to attract new employees. Talent balancing will get these problems of "company chaos" under control so management can put its full attention on growth and profitability.

Talent balancing is a dynamic process and a unique mind set that incorporates analyzing the work, the hiring plan, the hiring process, and the management of the staff. It helps management improve productivity, while putting the emphasis on growth and profitability instead of having the ongoing problem of company chaos.

The talent balancing technique can be easily outlined in six key points:

1. Ascertain your needs
2. Explore your hidden talent pool
3. Recruit what you need
4. Build talent balancing into the recruiting process
5. Manage your talent
6. Control costs and chaos with talent balancing

Before a company can balance its talent it must determine what talent is needed to do the job. Initially this should be done without looking at the current talent pool. This will give management a good idea of the workload and headcount needed. The next step is to look at your current employees in depth to determine what they can really do or are capable of doing. Once you have done that, you will find holes in the organization and will need to recruit new talent. The rest of this book goes into great detail on how to do this, so if you are not a recruiter and have little human resources experience, do not panic. We will go through a step-by-step chronological process to find and hire those superstars you want for your organization. After these people are on board, you want to keep them, so in step five we will give you a twelve-step management program to

*If there is anything that a man can do well, I say let him do it. Give him a chance.*
—Abraham Lincoln

ensure that the staff will be happy and productive. Finally, we have some good information on hidden costs incurred during the company chaos stage that you should be aware of at all times. Once you use the talent balancing techniques outlined in this book, this cost should be greatly reduced. We now take each one of these six steps and define them.

## 1. ASCERTAIN YOUR NEEDS

The first step in balancing your talent is to determine your actual needs. Some companies have the wrong talent for the direction they are going in or have never had the correct team in place to be able to be successful. In order to correct these problems, they typically add additional staff. Without knowing what is really needed this "solution" never works. Although people are usually matched to narrow job descriptions, they really need to be attached to the entire job. In order to be successful, they must go beyond the conventional job description, which can never include all of their abilities. In order to ascertain your needs, you should address the following matters:

1. Analyze past successes and failures
2. Consider future direction
3. Interview staff to determine where support is lacking

### Analyze Past Successes and Failures

If you look at each situation closely, you will probably be able to determine why you succeeded or failed. Look for the attributes of the successes. How were they structured? How was the team put together? What were the personality traits of the team players? What were their backgrounds? Why did some fail? What could have been done to make them successful? Were there too many people? Were there too few? What could you have done to make the teams more efficient? What were the essential attributes of the team leaders? How did they motivate the rest of the team? Were there outside forces affecting the outcome? Analyze this information and create a list of "bullets."

### Consider Future Direction

If you are changing corporate direction, it is necessary to establish a list of the new talent that you will need. The sales, marketing, and/or program managers can assist in creating this list. Some of these employees may have experience with the new product or services that could assist you in the formulation of a new department or, at the very least, key positions needed elsewhere throughout the company.

### Interview Staff

Talk to the employees, especially the nonexempt staff. They will usually know where the bottlenecks are and where additional manpower is needed. At the same time, they may know better procedures that may get more work done in a shorter time frame. In addition, ask about additional equipment that would help any of the processes. Buying a used copier to put in the shipping area may be cheaper than having the clerk walk up to accounting ten times a day to make copies. Solutions like this have a tendency to improve morale also. First the shipping clerks get their work done sooner *and* someone is interested in their problems!

### When Downsizing Becomes Capsizing

In some sad situations, large layoffs are needed. Problems always occur when a company goes through downsizing. These problems can be so critical that they may end up damaging the company beyond repair. Management must thoroughly understand what exactly happens before and after a layoff. Some companies do not want to have numerous small layoffs, so they have one large layoff, which, if not carefully thought out, usually ends up letting too many leave.

After every layoff, people get nervous and scared. You end up with what is called "chain reaction turnover." Employees go out and look for new jobs, expedite their retirement, go into business for themselves, or get out of the industry. At any rate, ninety days after your planned ten percent layoff, you could be looking at the reality that twelve to fifteen percent of the staff has actually left.

Now you have a smaller staff looking at a larger workload than they used to have. The people who used to put in long hours are now

*By now, everybody has gotten the word: It is the people, stupid . . . not the widgets. You have been hearing the mantra; PEOPLE ARE OUR MOST IMPORTANT ASSET, growing continually louder throughout the corporate world.*

—Anonymous

leaving at five o'clock and productivity starts to plummet. As morale drops, it becomes more difficult to get the staff motivated.

## Preventing Capsizing

Once you have determined that you need to reduce your overhead, look at short-term alternatives such as across-the-board salary cuts. Most employees would rather have a ten percent salary reduction than a ten percent layoff. Consider hiring freezes and going outside for part-time or consulting help to reduce overhead. Analyze what everyone is doing and consider shifting some responsibilities in order to meet your new revenue goals quicker. Maybe you take sales support engineers and have them assist making initial sales calls or have some of the marketing staff do telemarketing. Determine whom you really need and who can be replaced. This will take some time so do not rush it. There are some people that always look like they are busy but who never get anything done. Figure out where the workload is going to shift after the layout and make sure that the people left will be able to handle it.

The next step is to look into other cost-saving measures, such as ordering minimum amounts of office supplies and other consumables. Investigate new dealers and distributors to find out if you can get these items at a better price than you have in the past. Curtail all and any expenditures that can be put on hold, such as new furniture, computers, printers, and the like.

One of your most important activities is to keep the lines of communication with your staff open at all times. Once you have created a recovery plan, share it with them. Not knowing is the major fear that drives people to leave. Some will automatically leave, but a lot will stick with you if you maintain communication. It is essential to hold status meetings with all the employees on a regular basis. Use these meeting to kill rumors and to get the staff involved in cost-cutting ideas.

When layoffs occur, it is very important for management to review all of the staff resumes and core competencies in order to determine the essential personnel to keep. A smaller work force needs to be multitalented in order to handle a larger workload.

## 2. EXPLORE YOUR HIDDEN TALENT POOL

### Placing Employees in a Box

Most people (especially management people) have a tendency to put others in boxes. that they can never escape; if they see them or hire them as a "title" or "position," they cannot see them in any other job. Being shortsighted hurts everyone. You may have a superstar in your company and not know it! This limits people's ability to grow and expand their experiences. It also makes them feel that they will have to leave the company in order to advance.

---

**Case Example 1-1: Administrative Assistant in a Box**

*An administrative assistant had been working for a company for over seven years. She started as an administrative assistant when she first came on board. She was in the same department, did the same work, and interfaced with the same people day after day. She supported technical writers and was taking college classes in tech writing and doing very well. When an opening came up for a junior tech writer, she applied. However, since she was always looked upon as an administrative assistant and the HR manager did not know she was taking classes, she was ignored. Management did not have the foresight to even let her go through the interview process. She was labeled, put in a box, and overlooked. Shortly afterward, she left the company to go to another organization that did hire her as a junior technical writer. After being there for over a year, she returned to the original company and took a new technical writer position that had opened up. Coming from the outside, everyone accepted her as a technical writer, forgetting that she used to be an administrative assistant. The only way she could get the position was to leave the company and come back.*

---

Now, there is always the problem of employees who want the new position and salary but do not want to work at or do what it takes to get there. Typically, these people can just handle the job they currently occupy. However, some people have the background, desire, and/or capability to move into new areas. So in order to determine your hidden talent pool, you must not place employees in a box. It is important to keep the lines of communication open with all employees to find out if they want to have new responsibilities.

You must be aware if they are attending college classes or working on certificates that may change the work that they are currently doing.

On the other hand, they may not even know that classes or certifications are available to them. The HR department should find out if there are any local classes available to employees in your industry. Since the advent of the Internet, there have been major advancements made in distance learning." Employees are no longer tied to the traditional teacher-classroom method of learning. Young working mothers can use the Internet to take classes at their own speed, and busy employees can still take courses over the Internet or via video and get certified.

Finally, talk to the employees' managers and peers and find out what they have to say about their work habits, goals, work ethic, and relationships. You have now taken the employees out of the box.

### *Your Hidden Talent Pool*

Now that you have established your needs, it is time to unveil your hidden talent pool. One of the best sources in revealing your hidden talent pool is in the pages of your employees' resumes and their references. When you hired them, you were looking for a specific set of talents and did not pay much attention to their other experiences. When re-reviewing their resumes you may have to read between the lines in order to determine their additional talents. Be sure to take note of their education. Some people have degrees in areas in which they are not working. This could be due to the fact that they tried the field and did not like it, or they never got an opportunity to do anything in that field. So it is important to discuss things like this with them. Look at the different companies they worked at to find out if they are large or small companies or even start-ups. If your employees like new companies, they may have an entrepreneurial sprit you could use on a new project. If they worked for larger companies, they may know more about formal policies and procedures than other people in your organization. If they moved around a lot, they may be having a problem finding exactly what they want to do. (Be aware that in this economy there have been many companies that have merged or gone bankrupt, so job hopping may not be the employee's fault.)

In their personnel file, you should have access to the references taken during the interview process. Usually only HR and the hiring manager have read the references because they are only looking for possible problems or confirmation that the candidate can do the job they want. But there is also information in these references that will give you additional data on the personality of the person. A former boss may have stated something like, "Mary filled in for me as manager when I was out of town." This may have meant nothing to HR when they hired her because they were not hiring her for a management job. On the contrary, there may be potential management material there but nobody knew it. You may also read something about the person being a good individual contributor but lacking supervisory or project talent. You may see some people are gravitating toward areas of management or leadership and other people moving toward areas of individual contribution, working less with teams, and not interested in management. Some may have tried management but did not like it.

There is nothing wrong with people who are happy with what they are doing and who do not want to move up the ladder. If they don't seem to have that drive, help open the door for them so they have opportunities for advancement that they may have been unaware of. If they are happy where they are, so be it. The goal is to have employees who are challenged and happy and want to stay with the company.

The final and most essential step in this process is to actually talk to the employees. Get to know what they like and don't like doing. Find out their goals and ambitions. Because resumes are so short and only contain summary information, you must find out more detail about what the employees did in the past. Find out about as many of their experiences as you can. Determine what they want for the present and what they want for the future. Be sure to have your questions from the resume and reference check review and take notes. This process will be time consuming, but it is imperative that you find out how your talent pool looks before you start hiring new employees. When you are finished, you should write up a short summary for each employee and determine the following:

- Are they currently in the correct position?
- Are there other positions for which they would be better suited?
- Should they be positioned for a new position?
- Will they work well in a transition phase?
- In what positions can you use them as backups?
- Are they ready for training or mentoring?
- Should they not be working for your organization?

The Internet has a new activity now called "blogging." A blog is simply a journal (personal, corporate, political, topical, educational, legal, etc.) that is available on the web. The person who keeps a blog is a "blogger." The term "blogging" is defined as the activity of updating

*Many individuals have, like uncut diamonds, shining qualities beneath a rough exterior.*

—Anonymous

a blog. Blogs are typically updated daily using software that allows people with little or no technical background to update and maintain the blog on a web site. Reading blogs may be an excellent method of seeing the employee's likes and dislikes and how they approach the workplace.

### The Transition Phase

Employees in transition should be told that they may have to do some short-term projects that they may not like doing or appear to be beneath them. This may be necessary during the transition phase of growth and bringing on new staff.

Some people have a difficult time going through transitions and some do not know what to expect when they take a new position or get promoted. It is an especially big jump from the level of "individual contributor" to "manager." Most people do not know what to expect until they are already in the position, and by then it may be too late.

---

### Case Example 1-2: The Demoted Manager

*A new manager was brought in to take over for the current manager, who had been promoted from being an individual contributor into the manager's position, but apparently could not do the job. The company decided to demote the manager back to being an individual contributor and to look outside the company for a new manager. The HR department warned the incoming manager that the demoted manager might be difficult or become a troublemaker. After he came on board, the new manager met with the demoted manager. The first thing out of the demoted manager's mouth was, "Boy, I sure am glad you are here! I didn't know that being a manager meant doing so much paperwork and having to listen to all the staff's personal problems!" He turned out to be one of the biggest supporters of the new manager and never caused a problem.*

---

### Eliminate What You Do Not Need

After you have determined what you need and investigated the hidden talents in your organization, you must eliminate the people you no longer need. Layoffs are always tough. Nevertheless, you cannot carry people who do not produce; they will also drag down the people who do produce.

## 3. RECRUIT WHAT YOU NEED

So far, we have evaluated what talent is needed, explored the hidden talent pool, and removed staff that was not needed. We have now reached the point of the recruiting process: hiring what you need. Since the remainder of this book goes into the precise detail of the recruiting process, this chapter just covers the guidelines.

First, it must be determined if it is better to hire full-time people, part-time people, or outsource the current openings. The two primary factors in deciding are how long the activities are needed and what will be the costs. If you have a one-time project, then going outside is obvious. For example, you may have a project that needs to be established by a heavyweight consultant but then can be run by a junior worker and only use the consultant for emergencies. Part-time help is good when you have work that does not need a full forty hours a week to complete. There is the also the advantage of not having to pay benefits or overtime to part-time workers. Another process that works well is "temp to perm," where the company basically hires a person on a part-time basis, then, if it is discovered that the position needs to be permanent and the worker fits the company, they can be upgraded to full-time status. This gives the company the advantage to trying before buying.

### The Hiring Frenzy

The first problem that many companies encounter is a "hiring frenzy"—they hire people who end up being underutilized and after a few months end up frustrated, leaving, or being abandoned to layoffs. Hiring managers often make the initial mistake of hiring staff to solve today's problems, and not looking past the current projects. This trap is easy to fall into when everyone is coming at you with different needs and tasks that have to be solved—now. Even in the heat of battle, hiring managers must look beyond their day-to-day challenges to map out the ongoing needs of the department or team.

Before even submitting a staff requisition request or sketching out a job description, you should ask yourself, "What are the next three major projects that my staff should be working on? How many people do I really need to complete and support these projects? If the current project goes away, where would I put this person?" Beyond the personnel and project issues, you need to consider such factors as insurance, furniture, computers, space, equipment, and the other overhead to support a new hire such as staff in HR, accounting, MIS, facilities, and management departments. You should also consider the possibility of hiring people to fill immediate, temporary needs, and then loaning them out or transfering them to other departments, projects, or teams.

Ultimately, when interviewing candidates, beyond determining their fit for current projects and positions, you need to discuss their backgrounds and accomplishments in depth. The bottom line is to find out where a candidate's talents can be applied; most talented people are capable of learning new skills and responsibilities, and can adapt to changing circumstances. In the case of having temporary needs, you may bring talented people in at much lower cost than consultants or temporary workers, and then channel them into new projects or positions. Or alternatively, you may find temporary work for talented candidates in order to snag them, and then move them into a more permanent position as that project or department ramps up. Always plan for both present and future workloads.

---

### Case Example 1-3: Balancing Talent with Workload

*A computer company in its third year of operation and second round of funding was looking for a component engineer, although they were not yet in production. They decided to engage a recruiting consultant to help fill the position. When asked by the consultant why they needed someone a full year before production was slated to begin, the hiring managers explained that they wanted someone to set up their drawings, create a component library, organize and file the drawings, establish component specifications and relationships with vendors, and then manage the transition into production. They were adamant that they needed a full-time person to begin immediately. An ideal candidate was found. In sixty days, he had all the prep work completed. After that, he sat in his office, attended staff meetings, and drank coffee. After ten months, with production delayed, the company ended up laying off this engineer. Moral of the story: If you do not have the work, do not hire! Keep your talent balanced with the workload. Hire and keep staff based upon ongoing, long-term needs.*

---

### Controlling the Frenzy

Before submitting a staff requisition request, hiring managers should ask themselves, "What are the next three major projects that my staff should be working on?" and "How many people do I really need to complete and support these projects?" In addition, they should ask, "If the current project goes away, where would I put this person?" If you have a difficult time answering these questions, it may be better to hire consultants to do some of the short-term (three to four months) projects. After the consultant has completed the project, the consultant should cross-train one or two of your staff in order to learn and sustain the project. The consultant can them be "let go" and only used for emergency support situations in order that your department is not supporting an additional full-time person. Remember: the cost of a full-time person goes way beyond his or her salary. There are the overhead expenses noted in the section "The Hiring Frenzy."

*You put together the best team that you can with the players you've got, and replace those who aren't good enough.*
—Robert Crandall, Senior Fellow of Economic Studies, Brookings Institution

Good people will get bored if you do not keep them professionally challenged and will end up leaving, or they may be laid off because the company cannot support their expensive salaries. If there is not a current project in your department, consider "loaning" your talent (on a temporary basis) to another department. It may be possible to have one of your staff help another department or sister organization. In order to loan out talent, you must know everything that they can do.

Talented people with more than a few years of experience probably will not have everything they have accomplished on their two-page resume. In addition, during the interview, it was more important to find out if they could handle the primary project for which you were hiring. In order to determine their real capabilities, it is essential to sit down and discuss the candidates' backgrounds and accomplishments in depth.

Determine what expertise they have which can be used in other departments of the organization or how they can assist in short-term projects. Be sure to let the employees know that this is a temporary situation and that they are not being moved into another position. Maybe your development staff can assist the IT group in a conversion project that is just starting. Alternatively, maybe they can help

---

**Companies Buying Talent**

51% have an even balance between buying and building talent

23% rely on new hires

26% rely on developing talent from within

*Source:* "Companies Hold on to Their Cash," *Workforce Management Magazine,* December 2004, p. 105.

---

train the sales and/or support group on that complex product just released or work with marketing on new products. Some technical people may be used to talk to technical staff of your customer base to assist with the next generation of products or to determine possible product shortcomings. The same can be said for other department such as accounting or HR. You may be able to move that bright accounting clerk over to HR to help with performance reviews and salary increases.

The bottom line is to find out where else your top talented people can assist in the organization until their next major project is ready to start. Most of them are capable of learning new programs and responsibilities. In the end, it will be cheaper to get them to help than to hire consultants or to replace them because they were bored and left.

Another positive result of talent balancing is that if layoffs do come, some of your people may have other departments and positions to go to because they have already proven themselves. It will also allow you to have a smaller organization that is more efficient and less vulnerable to downsizing.

## 4. BUILD TALENT BALANCING INTO THE RECRUITING PROCESS

It is important to recruit exactly what you need, while observing the hidden talents of the candidates for future reference. In addition, it is important to bring on people who fit the corporate culture.

So what is corporate culture? It is basically the personality of a company. Some corporate cultures are expressed in their mission statement or company goals. Corporate culture is the company's ethics, core values, and beliefs. It is how management treats employees and how employees treat each other. Once you understand what your corporate culture is, you will be able to determine how candidates will fit into it. Fitting into the corporate culture is one if the most important aspects to consider when hiring.

## Outsourcing

Evaluating the time frame for some of your projects is important in order to determine if you need to outsource them. One of the key parameters is to decide if the project is going to be long-term or short-term. It may be easier, faster, more efficient, and save money to outsource short-term projects. In addition, it is essential to decide whether or not the project is one that has peaks and valley of activity. There is nothing worse than paying a large salary to staff who have nothing to do. If you do not have the expertise in-house and it is going to be expensive for you to recruit the talent needed, outsourcing may be the answer.

## Balancing the Organization and Workload

In order to continue your balancing, it is important to know your workload and organization. Morale will really be dragged down if some of the staff are working seventy hours a week and the rest are doing little or nothing. Find out where the bottlenecks are located, who has the best talents for the jobs to be performed, and balance the workload. You may have to reorganize what is left of your organization into a new structure that can handle the workload. It is important to communicate to the entire staff that some of the changes will be temporary and others may turn out to be permanent. But for the present, it is imperative that the talent be re-evaluated and redirected to ensure that the company will stay in business and be profitable.

## Growing Your Own

Looking at the future, the concept of growing your own talent should be considered. This concept consists of looking for those bright people who have little experience but a lot of drive. It will take a little time to get these people to a mature level of functionality, but they typically are very loyal and worth the wait. You have the satisfaction that you have trained them to your standards and, since they started at a lower level, they have a better grasp of how the company runs from the ground up. Be sure to keep their salaries level on a par with comparable positions in the industry, otherwise you may lose them to a fast-talking recruiter waving a fifteen percent increase under their noses.

## 5. MANAGING YOUR BALANCED TALENT

Having the best talent in the world will not help you if it is not managed properly. A very important concept of this book is this one on managing the talent. Listed below are the twelve steps to successful management.

### The Twelve-Step Reality Management Technique

1. Set the attitude
2. Communicate
3. Have a plan
4. Define staff and responsibilities
5. Provide the tools
6. Delegate and monitor
7. Handle change
8. Coach and mentor
9. Be honest
10. Be visible and approachable
11. Manage from respect
12. Maintain a sense of humor

### Step 1: Set the Attitude

If you are in management, everyone in your organization is continually evaluating your mood. They are listening to what you say and how you say it. They watch you, study your body language, listen to rumors about you, and create their "image" of you. This is the way people in a company try to find out what is happening at the management level. A company's attitude is reflected by its leaders. It is essential to establish open communications with everybody. They will follow your demeanor and reflect it.

Conversely, if you do not talk, keep your door closed, are always irritable and negative, the staff will start reflecting those emotions. If you, the leader, are positive, optimistic, encouraging, open, and an effective communicator, you will be establishing the attitude and example for the entire company.

A company with a positive attitude is capable of great success; a company with a negative attitude is doomed. If a company has gone through financial losses and layoffs, it may be difficult to keep hope alive, but this is exactly what is needed at this time.

The bottom line is that you do not want your staff to worry about your worrying. You want to take all obstacles out of their way by showing them how positive you are and how you trust that they can do the job. If the company feels that management is in control, has a positive outlook, and is solving problems, the working staff can stop worrying and can go back to getting the job done.

> *The first task of a leader is to keep hope alive.*
> —Joe Batten,
> business author

### Step 2: Communicate

This section on communications falls into two categories: research communications and the actual communications link.

#### Research Communications
As an effective leader, it is important to get the input of all involved in the decision making process. You may be good, but you still need a staff, and the best staff is one that assists in the analysis and final decisions. If the staff has been included in the "research," they typically will support the final plan.

#### Communications Link
Effective communications is one of the most important keys to successful management. Habits that should be developed in order to maintain accurate and efficient communication are as follows:

##### Getting Another's Attention
Before you can talk to someone, you must get their attention, so they know you are addressing them. I know this sounds pretty simple, but many miscommunications occur when one of the parties does not know they are being addressed.

##### Talking
Now that you have someone's attention, you can start the conversation. Make sure that you have already thought out what you are going to say before you say it. Some people start in the middle of their thought process and instantly confuse the listener. Also, make sure that you can be easily heard. Do not speak too softly. When you have completed your thought, pause to see if the listener heard and understood you.

Figure 1-1

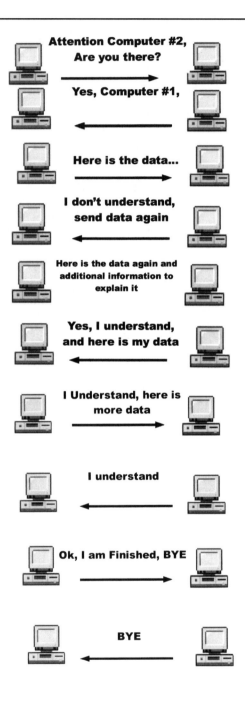

*Listening*

When someone is talking, concentrate on what they are saying and do not focus on what you are going to say in response. Wait until they have completed their thought and pause for your response. As soon as they do, acknowledge them. It should be noted that some people try to control the conversation by interrupting with acknowledgments. They do this in order to stop you. When more than one acknowledgment occurs, the other person usually feels that they have not finished their thought and so they just keep repeating themselves. The communications link has now broken down and the speaker does not feel the other person cares about them.

> *The art of communication is the language of leadership.*
> —James Humes, author and speechwriter for five U.S. presidents

It has been said that one of President Ronald Reagan's greatest attributes was his ability to listen. They say that when he was listening to you talk, it felt like you were the only person in the room.

*Responding*

If you did not understand a word, concept, or intention, ask the speaker to repeat it until you comprehend what was said. Do not hope that later in the conversation you will figure out what they said. Your mind will become preoccupied with the misunderstanding and start missing other stated information.

Computers are programmed like this in order to be able to transmit large masses of information with no mistakes or misunderstandings (see figure 1-1).

**Informing The Troops**

Keeping all employees informed is the foundation of great leadership. Companies that have monthly meetings with all employees keeps the morale up and the workers feeling that they are part of a team. E-mails and company newsletters are also good, but face-to-face communication is the best.

---

*Case Example 1-4: Keeping Employees Informed*

*A fast-growing company needed a method of keeping the employees up-to-date with the latest activities in the organization. They decided to have all-hands meetings. They would bring in lunch for everybody on the first Friday of every*

> *Leadership is a matter of having people look at you and gain confidence, seeing how you react. If you're in control, they're in control.*
>
> —Tom Landry, former head coach of the Dallas Cowboys

month. *During lunch, they would have HR make announcements (HR always has something to address) and then the president would give a positive, informational, and short presentation on what was going on, new contracts, new developments, and so on. At the end of every fiscal quarter, management would hand out quality corporate giveaways, such as calculators, golf shirts, key chains, and so on, to all the employees after the meeting. This company also had a bonus program for all employees. Fifty percent of it was based on department or corporate objectives and the other fifty percent based on individual contribution. At the same time every year, the CFO would distribute all the checks at the end of the all-hands meeting in alphabetical sequence. As the individual employee received his or her check, the rest of the organization clapped and congratulated the staffer. Internal public relations was always at a high level and employees always felt they were part of a team and rewarded for their efforts.*

Communication—the listening and dissemination of information—is the foundation of Reality Management™.

### Step 3: Have a Plan

Once you have established a "can-do" attitude with open communications, you must present a plan (or an interim plan) that has realistic goals. This is especially important when there have been major changes in the company or industry. People want to know that their leader is watching out for them and the company and will fight hard to keep layoffs from occurring. Even the janitors and shipping clerks want to know that their leader is proactive and knows what to do.

A true leader tells the organization that a plan is being worked on, develops one, and then disseminates it to everyone. If employees know that there are problems, and they do not see or hear anything happening to address them, morale starts to drop like a rock, soon to be followed by a drop in productivity, and, finally, people start leaving for other jobs.

---

### Case Example 1-5: Disseminate the Plan

*The president of a small division of a major aerospace firm is told by corporate that they are going to reorganize the division by product, in effect splitting them in two. Half will be moved down the road to a new facility and the other half will remain in their present facility. Instead of putting a plan together to do this and then disseminating it to the division, the president called an all-hands meeting and told everybody what was going to occur. When asked when it was going to happen, who was going to be affected, and how it was going to be handled, all he could say was, "I don't know." It took only a ten-minute meeting to scare or anger almost all of the employees of the organization. Many of those who had been there for a long, long time went home and updated their resumes.*

---

In the creation of the plan, it is important that key staff members and anyone else who can supply relevant information assist with the plan in order for the company to become a team that pulls together. The goal(s) may be difficult, but they should always be realistic so the organization feels they can be accomplished. If the goals are really impossible, people will lose faith and stop pushing because deep in each heart, they know they cannot do it.

It is important to use the plan to make decisions. Presidents who do not make decisions because they are worried about being wrong never get anything accomplished. Staff watching this feels that these presidents are not making decisions because they do not think the problem is important or that it deserves an answer. This makes the staff feel that their problems are unimportant.

### Step 4: Define Staff and Responsibilities

#### Defining Staff

By using talent balancing techniques, you can discover the additional talents of the current staff. Using this information, you must ask the following questions:

1. What activities can be performed inside and what activities are better taken outside?
2. Who can handle different and/or new responsibilities?

*Lead, follow or get out of the way!*

—Anonymous

> *Opportunity without the proper tools is like a cart without a horse.*
>
> —Anonymous

3. How should the new inside organized be structured?
4. What temporary activities are needed?
5. What new hires need to be obtained and where do they fit?
6. Have you discussed the changes with the staff individually?
7. Have you defined all the responsibilities and authority?

If you have tasks that will only take a few months to do, or you do not have the expertise to complete them easily inside, outsourcing should be considered. When you hire staff full time, not only are you paying salary you also are paying for benefits, insurance, computers, desks, chairs, office supplies, and so on. Going outside you only pay for the project or hours to do the project. When it is over, you are not carrying a full-time person or having to lay them off. The financial trade-off is obvious after you determine what has to be done. For example, it may be determined that outside services can be used to create foundations policies and procedures, then a less experienced (i.e., less costly) full-time employee(s) can be hired to just run the department.

The next step is to review your current employees' resumes to understand other activities they may be qualified to do. Some may be beneath what they are doing now. When you are assigning your staff to work on these projects temporarily, they should be totally aware that it is temporary and, if possible, a time frame should be estimated. If employees do not understand this, they may think that they are being punished for some reason.

Some employees may be capable of handling new areas. If you have an organizational problem in one department, you may have a manager in another department who is a great organizer, and who may be able temporarily to transfer to the problem department and get it organized.

The company should be organized so that the proper managers are in the key spots and the support staff is effective but lean. Traditional line and staff management structure works best.

> *Ability is of little account without opportunity.*
>
> —Anonymous

All of the employees must know whom they report to, who reports to them, and what their responsibilities and goals are. They must know who has authority and how the chain of command works. Everyone should know their signing authority and whom to report problems to when they cannot solve them.

### Defining Responsibilities

Building a team that can carry out the corporate plan is key to a successful organization. Responsibility and authority must be properly balanced. One without the other always will cause problems.

There is an unsuccessful management technique being used wherein one particular job will be given to two or more people. The idea behind this concept is that "if I give the problem to enough people, someone will solve it!" Nothing upsets an employee more than being part of this maneuver.

## Step 5: Provide the Tools

It is essential always to provide everyone with the best tools available to do their tasks. You do not have to go overboard with the use of current technology, but there are a lot of good tools now available and you should be generous with them. It is very frustrating for the staff not to be able to meet their goals because they have poor or obsolete tools.

## Step 6: Delegate and Monitor

Leaders must delegate the proper responsibilities to the correct people and then let everyone else in the company know who is accountable for what tasks. This will eliminate the problem of two or more people trying to do the same thing or staff not knowing who is responsible for key functions. Once responsibilities have been established, the leader must never, ever, attempt to micromanage a project. The major complaints that most employees have about their boss is that they either try to run everything or that they do not inform them of responsibilities or changes in policy or direction until it is too late. As a leader you must also monitor the key activities in the company. This can be done through meetings, reports, verbal updates, e-mails, and so on.

## Step 7: Handle Change

A recent survey revealed that one of the top five complaints that staff had about management was that they continually changed directions.

*I don't want to work for any company where intelligence is optional.*

—Anonymous

Direction changing sends out mixed messages and reveals that you probably do not know what you are doing. This does not mean that you cannot change your plans when necessary, but you must avoid numerous changes in short periods in time. If you are making numerous changes in direction, there must be a major problem with your business plan or base assumptions about your business. Your staff will eventually just stop working because very shortly you will change your mind and all their previous work will be for nothing anyway. This is one of the most important of the twelve rules.

### Step 8: Coach and Mentor

An effective leader uses the methodology of a coach and mentor to educate, encourage, and correct the staff. Done correctly, the staff will grow and learn from their mistakes instead of trying to hide them and/or blame others. It is very important to give employees meaningful recognition when it has been deserved.

### Step 9: Be Honest

In business (as in life), honesty is not an option, especially when you are a leader and have an entire company looking up to you and the standards you establish. Your honesty defines your character and credibility. Honesty in business is essential. Promises must never be broken and all activities should be above board and out in the open.

### Step 10: Be Visible and Approachable

The president in our case example 1-6 below was neither visible nor approachable. Because of this, the staff started feeling that they were neither important nor wanted. The effective leader comes into the office in the morning and walks through the entire area greeting and talking to everyone.

*If you don't stand for something, you'll fall for anything*

—Michael Evans, author

This should be done at least once a day. It is also an excellent idea to go through the office again in the evening, say, after six or six-thirty to see who is working after hours and why. Always try to keep your office door open and see anyone who wants to talk to you. If you are in the middle of something, have them make an appointment or better yet go to them when you can.

> 61% of the nation's workers said they have not received meaningful recognition in the last year
>
> *Source:* Gallup Organizational Polls 2004

---

### *Case Example 1-6: The Invisible President*

*A small (staff of 50) start-up company had a president who rarely would come out of his office. Few saw him when he arrived in the morning and even fewer would see him leave at night. The rest of upper management suggested that they have a monthly all-hands lunch/meeting. The president would update the staff on news of the company, potential customers, new customers, and so on. Then they would serve the catered lunch. It was a great idea, except after the president gave his (always short) pitch, he would not take any questions, and would be first in line for the food. After loading up his plate, he would then go back to his office and eat by himself leaving the rest of the company downstairs. This is not a leader, and consequently the company eventually went bankrupt.*

---

## *Step 11: Manage from Respect*

Anyone can manage by fear and intimidation and it will work for a short period of time. But the good people will move on, the deadwood will put up with it, but you will never develop an efficient, self-motivated team. It is essential to manage from respect in order to have a well-run organization.

## *Step 12: Maintain a Sense of Humor*

Business today is fast paced, demanding, challenging, stressful, and intense. The best way to combat anxiety and stress is to keep a sense of humor about any situation and be able to laugh at yourself. Great men in history became even greater when they showed the human side of themselves through humor. Remember, those Dilbert cartoons are closer to reality than you could ever imagine!

> *There is no twilight zone of honesty in business; it is either right or wrong!*
> —John Dodge, editor and publisher

*Familiarity breeds credibility,*
*credibility breeds loyalty,*
*loyalty breeds teamwork.*
—Jim Stedt

**Case Example 1-7: A Sense of Humor**

*The CEO of a multibillion dollar East Coast computer corporation was on an inspection tour of one of their facilities in California. Everyone in the facility was dressed up and there was a feeling of formality and stiffness in the air. When the CEO came out onto the production floor, everyone held their breath because they did not expect him to be out there. Since the CEO came up the ranks as an engineer himself, he wanted to see the hardware being built and tested. A young product manager boldly stepped up and started explaining the testing process. The CEO stared at the equipment and calmly asked "Why was the smaller printer faster than the larger printer?" The product manager thought for a second and quipped, "Since it is in a smaller space, the data wants to get out faster!" Everyone in the area laughed and all of a sudden you could feel them all relaxing. After that, the CEO took his coat off, sat on a computer table, and told stories of when he was an engineer. Later, the California facility heard from corporate that the CEO enjoyed his trip there best because the people there had a great sense of humor.*

## 6. CONTROL COSTS AND CHAOS WITH TALENT BALANCING

Company chaos is defined as all of the new problems that you must fix because you did not handle the baseline problems properly. For example, management must be aware of the high cost of turnover. If your organization is becoming a revolving door for employees, you are losing at lot of money, knowledge, and valuable time. When an employee leaves for any reason, the company will suffer financial losses. Some of these are obvious, direct costs and some are hidden costs. If you have hired too many people too fast or your sales forecasts are not met, you may have to face the fact you must have layoffs of personnel. This adds to the revolving door problem. After a while, your company gets a reputation for going through people and not being focused on keeping staff. A lot of companies do not realize the added costs of layoffs, employee searches, or hiring.

## Layoff Costs

Once you have gone through the layoff process, you need to evaluate the losses you have incurred. They include direct and hidden layoff costs. Direct layoff costs include the following:

> *Humor is the absence of terror, and terror the absence of humor.*
> —John Cleese, actor, writer, and director

- Immediate costs are the final paycheck, paid accrued vacation and for some companies, paid sick Leave. Most of these costs are paid within forty-eight hours of the layoff.
- Ongoing costs are extended severance pay and Insurance for key employees. Some upper-echelon staff will be given severance pay and have their insurance paid for six to twelve months.
- Increased unemployment tax to the company must be paid.
- Some companies will incur outplacement costs to provide these services to some of their staff.

Hidden layoff costs include the following:

- Administrative costs for paperwork for the HR department
- Exit interviews and transition meetings costs
- IT and facilities costs for removing or relocating cell phones, changing passwords, e-mail, computers, PDAs, and so on
- Lower productivity due to reduced manpower and reduced morale at company
- Overtime or extended hours for the employees who remain

Talent balancing techniques will help reduce or eliminate the staff reduction problem.

## Search Costs

Search costs include direct and hidden candidate search costs. Direct costs for a candidate search include:

- Employee referral program costs. Some companies pay their employees a referral fee for candidates that are hired. These fees may be from one hundred to thousands of dollars, depending on the company.

| Working Retention Tools |
| :---: |
| 59% Competitive Merit Increase |
| 57% Promotion |
| 50% Career Development Opportunity |
| 41% Bonuses |
| 28% Flex-time |
| 7% Stock Options |
| 2% Enhanced Retirement Packages |

Source: Andrew Dietz, "Talent-Management Boom Could Be Good for You," November 2002. Available at http://www.CareerJournal.com/ columnist/20021104fmp.html. Accessed March 2005.

- Search firm/recruiter costs. Retained search, contract recruiters, and contingency search firms will charge anywhere from ten percent to forty percent of the first year's compensation.
- Advertising and job fair costs. Advertising in major newspapers and trade publications typically can run into the thousands of dollars. If the company attends job fairs, there are costs involved in travel, booth space, lost time for people out of the office, and collateral materials.
- Reference checks, credit checks, background checks, and the like. Once an offer is ready to be presented to a candidate, reference checks have to be made. This cost will either be paid to an outside service or the time will be taken by an in-house employee.
- Medical exams and drug tests costs.
- Temporary/contract employee costs may be sustained.

Hidden costs for a candidate search include:

- Lost time by hiring managers, staff and HR for resume screening, interviews and staffing meetings
- Administrative support costs

## Hiring and Orientation Costs

Hiring and orientation costs include direct and hidden costs and corporation losses. Direct hiring and orientation costs include:

- Relocation costs
- Orientation materials
- Formal training programs
- Cost of furniture, computer, office supplies, land-based and cell phones, business cards, and so on

- IT costs to set up new computer, e-mail, PDA, passwords, and the like
- Facilities cost to prepare office and phone

Hidden hiring and orientation costs include:

- Lost productivity of HR, IT, and facilities staff
- Informal training and one-on-ones

Corporation losses due to hiring and orientation include:

- Missed deadlines and shipments
- Loss of organization knowledge ("hall talk")
- Additional workload for staff left after layoff
- Learning curve for new staff
- Client problems not solved during transition time
- Possible damaged client relationships
- Disrupted corporate operations
- Lower morale of current staff
- People leaving after a layoff ("chain reaction turnover")

### No Cooks OR Broth

Some companies have too many cooks spoiling the broth. Other companies do not have cooks or broth. These companies are continually understaffed and cannot do a good, high-quality, productive job. The people that are in this type of company are usually overworked and stressed out. Morale is low because the staff can see no end or solution in sight. This type of company trudges along, not wanting to increase head count, but wanting to grow. The fact of the matter is that they cannot have it both ways.

### No Cooks OR Broth Corrective Action

In order to do a good job, management must realize that they must support their organization with the manpower to complete the tasks. In order to do this, upper management should sit down with the key employees and learn from them where the shortcomings are in the system. Many times they find out that just adding a few new administrative staffers frees up the key workers to do the real productive,

*Nothing is impossible for the person who does not have to do it themself.*

—Anonymous

moneymaking tasks. Another concept is to hire interns and/or part-time help to test the workload to determine its size. It will initially cost more money but the return will make up for it, and is typically quicker than you might think. The increased morale will be noticed as soon as the new staff starts.

## Improved Communications

Improving your internal communications will help eliminate the chaos that you have in your company. Chaos is typically the result of the employees not knowing what the priorities, responsibilities, processes, or lines of authority are in the company. Defining these areas and communicating them to the entire company will help eliminate the "not knowing." When people don't know something, they guess at it or make it up so they can move on. The results are that no one knows what is going on and problems beget problems. Improving communications and keeping the staff up to speed on all the changes will help eliminate the chaos in your organization.

## Balanced Workload

Once you have evaluated what has to be done and confirmed the talent needed to do it, you are on your way to creating a balanced workload. This will allow you to keep costs down and morale up. It is difficult to watch some people work eight hours a day and other people work fourteen hours a day. There will be times when this will naturally occur, but it should be only for a short period or during a crisis.

## SUMMARY

Some leaders have a natural charisma and are born to lead. The rest of us have to work at it. We must follow these twelve rules carefully and maintain a leadership decorum that gathers respect from our staff. It is essential to follow these rules at all times. If you have just one bad day and you take it out on your staff, it will take a while to get them back up. After you work at these rules for a while, they will become part of you. Your staff will work with you and enjoy success as much as you do. The bottom line is to create a team that does high-quality work, within budget, and within the allotted time frame. A true leader can do this by following these steps.

Talent balancing can improve productivity, save labor costs, improve morale, and build a strong team. You can hire and keep staff based on ongoing, long-term needs and on using your department staff for more than their original recruited roles. You can also "grow your own" staff to meet your own standards. When you master these concepts, you can keep your staff smaller, postpone layoffs, and create a lean and meaningful organization. The key is to know your actual workload, your "on-board talent," their challenges, and their potential.

**Form 1-1**
**Talent Balancing Checklist**

---

**1  Ascertain Your Needs**
❑ Analyze past successes and failures
❑ Consider future direction
❑ Determine the workload

**2  Explore Your Hidden Talent Pool**
❑ Interview one-on-one
❑ Interview managers
❑ Interview peers
❑ Interview HR
❑ Read staff blogs

**3  Recruit What You Need**
❑ Determine talent needs
❑ Evaluate what is available and what must be recruited
❑ Eliminate "deadwood"

**4  Building Talent Balancing into the Organization**
❑ Building it into the recruiting process
❑ Planning for the future
❑ Improving the management process

**5  Managing Your Balanced Talent**
❑ Twelve-Step Reality Management Technique
   1. Set the attitude
   2. Communicate
   3. Have a plan
   4. Define staff and responsibilities
   5. Provide the tools
   6. Delegate and monitor
   7. Handle change
   8. Coach and mentor
   9. Being honest
   10. Be visible and approachable
   11. Manage from respect
   12. Maintain a sense of humor

*(continued)*

**Form 1-1**
**Talent Balancing Checklist** *Continued*

**6 Controlling Costs and Chaos with Talent Balancing**
❏ Costs
    Layoff costs
    Search costs
    Hiring and orientation costs
❏ Improved communications
❏ Balanced workload

# CHAPTER 2
## Basics of Successful Recruiting

In this book we are addressing the independent recruiter consultant, the corporate recruiter, or anyone involved with hiring. The basics and the goals are the same for any of these situations. In consulting, recruiting has evolved from a service to a profession and clients are expecting professional behavior and results.

### QUALITIES OF THE SUCCESSFUL RECRUITER

As companies go through difficult economic times and let full-time recruiters go, the other HR personnel inherit the responsibility of the corporate recruiter. Most HR people do not enjoy recruiting, so it is the last to get any attention. But as companies start enjoying better economic times, it is necessary to start hiring again. In early economic recovery, it may not be possible to hire a full-time recruiter or consultant. This leaves the recruiting responsibility up to others in the HR department. So if you are an HR professional, but lack recruiting skills, this is an important chapter for you.

#### Career Counseling and a Passion to Help

The successful recruiter does more than just bring candidates through the door; they have a passion to help the hiring managers, the candidates, and the corporation.

The hiring manager needs a recruiter in order to meet department goals and eventually corporate goals. Most hiring managers are over-burdened, overworked, and under a great deal of stress. New staff can help them shift the workload and become more efficient. This typically will lead to the successful completion of tasks at hand.

The successful recruiter will provide candidates with a form of career counseling. By evaluating their background and determining if there is a potential for a good corporate culture fit, the recruiter can put the candidate on a great career path. On the other hand, if the match is not a good one, the recruiter will communicate this to the candidate in such a way that the candidate understands that if they got the job, it would not be good for them in the long run.

---

### Case Example 2-1: The Candidate with Reservations

*After a long search for the position of controller, the recruiter finally brought in an impressive candidate for an interview with the president and chief financial officer (CFO). The interviews went well with the candidate and she was very interested in the position. However, after the second round of interviews, she meekly revealed to the recruiter that she had just a hint of reluctance to go any further, but did not really know why. Subsequent talks with the president and CFO revealed a similar (but ever-so-slight) feeling. The recruiter advised them to "pass" on the candidate because if there was the slightest hint that the relationship would not work going into it, it would be doomed to failure. All parties took the recommendation of the recruiter and afterward everyone felt it was the right decision. The candidate thanked the recruiter for not pushing her into something for which she had unknown reservations that could not be verbalized.*

---

## Communications Focal Point

We have touched on the successful recruiter being a communications focal point. In today's business environment, staff members who work in cubicles right next to each other may not be communicating at all. Everyone is so wrapped up with their own work and projects they usually do not know what else is happening in the organization. It is the responsibility of the successful recruiter to keep all interested parties informed and up-to-date as to the activities, problems, outcomes, and changes in the recruiting process. This can be a difficult job due to the fact that some people do not like to read or return their e-mails or phone calls. It is essential to determine the most effective communications method for each of the key recruiting players. All communications must always be timely and accurate. If you do not know the answer to a question, say so. Never *guess* or give false information. If you do, it will cause all kinds of erroneous rumors and misinformation.

### Reactive and Proactive Recruiters

Over the last few years, recruiters have migrated into two categories: reactive and proactive. Reactive recruiters, typically corporate, only respond when resumes come to them. They usually do not drive the process: instead, they just forward the resumes and wait for a response, which may be corporate policy. Some companies use a system based on resume flow. The resume flows into the HR department and is directed to the proper hiring manager who, in turn, reviews it and either contacts the candidate for an interview or passes on it. If the hiring manager is too busy, the resumes stack up and may or may not be read. The recruiter will not get involved again until the candidate is brought in for an interview.

Proactive recruiters, on the other hand, seek out applicants and drive every step of the process to its ultimate conclusion. They even look for "passive candidates," people who are neither actively looking for a job, nor posting their resumes on the Internet, nor sending out resumes. They usually do not even have an up-to-date resume available.

The proactive recruiter also prepares a recruiting plan, which incorporates the use of the following: staffing time frame, number of open job requisitions, budget, type of openings, recruiting priorities, tools available, and step-by-step process attached to a time line. The exact details of a recruiting plan are covered in depth later in this chapter.

Proactive recruiters drive the step-by-step process, following the recruiting plan. When the process has stopped, proactive recruiters locate and solve the problems, then push the process to the next step. They make sure that all of the communications are occurring accurately and on time. They verify that all the paperwork, policies, and procedures are being handled and completed. Proactive recruiters insure that all parties know exactly what is going on and what is the next step that should be taken. A status report is generated every week or two to keep everyone "in the know," especially people who are not on the daily communications such as the president, CEO, CFO, and the like.

### Achieving Corporate Goals

The ultimate goal of the successful recruiter is to achieve corporate recruiting goals. If the company has done its business planning homework correctly, it will know who they need to hire to be successful and *when* to hire them. The successful recruiter knows that they must work within these parameters.

## THE STAFFING PLAN

The first step in the recruiting process is the design of an effective recruiting strategy. Many of these steps are explained in greater detail in chapter 6. In order to design an effective recruiting strategy, you must have knowledge of or implement the following steps:

- Know the industry
- Know the company and its corporate culture
- Find out the number of requisitions needed and types of openings
- Know projected hire dates
- Determine locations of hires
- Determine recruiting budget
- Implementation plan
- Managing your time
- Driving the process
- Interviews
- Negotiating the compensation package
- Making the offer
- New hire follow-up

### Know the Industry

If you are new to the industry, it is necessary to learn some of the basics. Most sales or marketing people can provide you with such information as the size and background of the industry, the competition, types of people and their average longevity in the industry, and current state of the industry (is it depressed, growing, stable?).

## Know the Company and Its Corporate Culture

It is important to know what type of corporate culture the company has and the work ethic that has evolved. Also, find out about the history of the company, the successes, and who the key people are in the organization. Inquire about the products and/or services provided by the company. Determine if there are other offices or divisions other than those at the corporate location. Being a recruiter is like being a sales person for the company, so the more you know about it the better. Of course, you also need to know about all of the perks and benefits available. Also find out about the little-known benefits like having monthly company pizza lunches or yearly parties. This all adds up when you are selling the company to the candidate.

You must also find out about the company's entire recruiting process. How are resumes handled? How does each hiring manager like to interview? What review forms (if any) are used? Who determines what the offer will be? Who must approve offers and offer letters? Are standard offers or employment contracts used? When are "no thank you" letters sent out and who does them? How are personnel files created?

## Number of Requisitions and Types of Openings

Next is to find out the number of openings and job titles. This is going to have a major impact on the timing of the recruiting plan. For example, it will probably take longer to find a chief technology officer than a controller. The requisitions will also have the salary range available for each position. Make sure you find out about any bonuses or commission plans available. In addition, some companies will have sign-on bonuses or will pay for relocation.

## Projected Hire Dates

Each job requisition will have a projected hire date. Some positions have to be filled before others, such as a manager who will be hiring staff. Once you hire the manager they can assist in hiring the rest of their organization. Other positions may be needed to be hired in sequence also such as hiring the sale force before hiring the customer support staff. The company's business plan or sales objectives should have this outlined. If not, make sure you always ask for the hiring priority. In some situations, hiring cannot be started until certain sales goals have been met. If this is true, you need to know the arrangement.

### Salary Compression Issues

As you recruit, you may find out that your company's salaries are lower than the current industry standard. You may have a salary compression problem, which occurs when the industry increases salaries but the company does not. A three or four percent increase per year for the company's annual increase may be less that what the industry has been increasing. If the company has not hired these positions in a while, they may be behind the industry curve. Salary compression problems will reveal themselves quickly when you start the recruiting process and two or three people tell you they are making fifteen percent more than you have to offer. The company should address this problem as soon as possible because they have the problem of bringing people into the organization that are making more money than someone who has been loyal and has been with the company for a number of years. It will be necessary to put in a fast-track salary program to get the company up to industry standards. Otherwise the company will start losing people when they find out they are being underpaid.

## Locations of Hires

If the company has multiple locations, you need to find out where the new hire will work. It is more difficult to hire for Chicago if you are located in Los Angeles and have no hiring assistance in Chicago. This will have an impact on your hiring time frame when you are creating the recruiting plan.

## Budget

Determine the hiring budget that you have available to you. Can you budget for job fairs, advertising, posting on the Internet, and hiring recruiting consultants or contingency search firms? Will you need a travel budget if you are hiring outside your location? Depending on the number of hires you have and the time frames, you may need some or all of these items budgeted.

## Implementation Plan

Once you have all of this information, you can put together your recruiting plan. Sometimes it is good to put together a time line chart or recruiting schedule to determine if there are any timing problems in implementing the plan (see figure 2-1). This should show you if need

Library, Nova Scotia Community College

Figure 2-1

| Recruiting Schedule | | | | | | | | | | | | | | | | |
| --- | --- | --- | --- | --- | --- | --- | --- | --- | --- | --- | --- | --- | --- | --- | --- | --- |
| **Week** 1 2 3 4 5 6 7 8 9 10 11 12 13 14 15 16 17 | | | | | | | | | | | | | | | | |
| **Positions** Acct Mgr | | | | | | | | | | | | | | | | |
| Accountant II | | | | | | | | | | | | | | | | |
| Payroll Analyst | | | | | | | | | | | | | | | | |
| Admin Asst | | | | | | | | | | | | | | | | |
| Marketing Director | | | | | | | | | | | | | | | | |
| Sales Manager | | | | | | | | | | | | | | | | |
| Administrator | | | | | | | | | | | | | | | | |
| Receptionist | | | | | | | | | | | | | | | | |

additional budget, time, or outside assistance. Make sure you raise any problems you see as soon as possible to management. The financial health of the company may depend on your activities!

### Managing Your Time

The recruiting process is difficult because there are so many things happening, especially when staffing a number of different positions. It is important to manage your time as much as possible. Make sure you have an accurate calendar to schedule phone interviews, in-person interviews, hiring manager follow-ups, and other key activities that you will be involved in. Do not leave anything to memory no matter how good your memory is. You do not want to make a mistake with a candidate or hiring manager. It may cost you the hire!

There will be situations in which you do not have the time to call the ten potential candidates you found on the Internet. When this happens, e-mail can be a real time saver. Send all of the candidates a copy of the job description, company information, and location of the position. If they are interested they will reply to the e-mail. This is an excellent method to expedite the job search. You usually do not know how long a resume has been posted on the Internet. Some Internet job banks pull resumes off of other sites so candidates may not even know where their resumes are placed. As a result, an applicant may already have a new position or may have decided not to continue the job search. E-mailing can help to rapidly determine client interest and save a lot of time in the search.

It is usually easier to make phone interviews during off hours (evenings or weekends) so the candidate can talk easily instead of trying to whisper in their cubicles at work. Some candidates will call you on their cell phones during a break or lunch when they are off the corporate premises.

Plan on setting aside some quiet time to review those resumes that are difficult to read or fall into that maybe category.

### Driving the Process

There are not many people who are interesting in the hiring process. They all have their own jobs to do and stopping them to recruit is at times frustrating to them. So it is up to the successful recruiter to drive the process whenever it appears that it has stopped or is being delayed. After sending the hiring managers resumes to review, make sure you follow up with them if they have not responded in a couple of days. Remember, the candidate will be talking to other companies so time is of the essence. Some hiring managers do not realize that they are in a race to place good people in their key positions and if they wait too long the company will lose the candidate. The recruiting process is greatly slowed down, and sometimes even stops.

After the in-person interview process is completed, the recruiter must contact each interviewer to determine their opinion of the candidate. If there appears to be confusion about an applicant's capabilities, suggest a second interview cycle in order to make a final decision. On the other hand, if they are interested in making an offer, the recruiter should make sure that the offer letter gets processed and, if necessary, schedule the drug test, medical test, and/or third party reference checks as soon as possible.

In this fast-paced business climate, it is easy for candidates to "fall through the cracks." When this happens, candidates do not feel respected and there is a good chance of losing them altogether. On the other hand, if they are kept informed and the recruiting process continues to move at a logical and brisk pace, candidates will feel good about signing that offer letter. The successful recruiter will drive the process to its logical end, keeping everyone informed of its status along the way.

## Interviews

The successful recruiter understands that the most critical of all of the recruiting processes is the interview. Interviews (either by phone or in person) are a combination of selling the company to the candidate and determining if the candidate's experience, chemistry, and corporate culture background will interconnect with the organization. Both parties are selling themselves in this step of the recruiting process.

## Negotiating the Compensation Package

One of the pivotal points in recruiting is negotiating the total compensation package. The successful recruiter will try to find out early in the recruiting cycle the desires of the candidate. It is important not to get too far into the process before this is done. If you have a budget of $75,000 and the candidate wants a minimum of $100,000 you may be wasting everybody's time. Some candidates are more interested in the challenge of the position while others look at salary first and foremost.

## Making the Offer

The successful recruiter should know exactly what it will take to get the candidate hired before making the offer. When the offer is finally made, the probability of the hire actually goes down because the candidate may have other offers, they may be brought back by their current company, or they may just have changed their mind.

## New Hire Follow-Up

After the candidate accepts the offer and becomes an employee, the successful recruiter will keep in close touch with the new hire for the first thirty to forty-five days. It is good internal PR to make sure that the new person becomes integrated into the company culture.

**Figure 2-2**

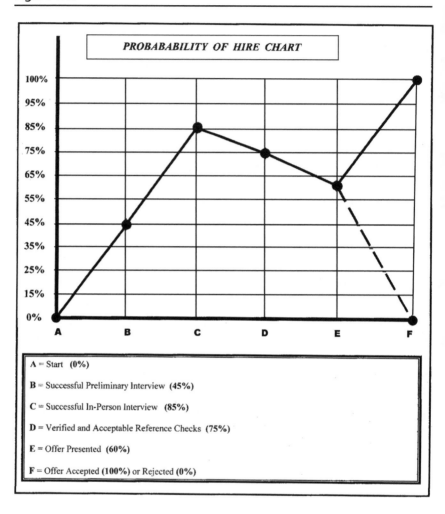

## THE PROBABILITY OF HIRE CHART

The recruiting process has six steps by which the probability of hire can be estimated (see figure 2-2):

- Start
- Successful Preliminary Interview
- Successful In-Person Interview
- Reference Check

- Offer
- Acceptance or Rejection of Offer

## 1. Start

When the search has just started, the probability level is at zero percent because there are no candidates in the cycle. This is the point at which the search begins, potential candidates are gathered, and preliminary interviews are started (figure 2-2A).

## 2. Successful Preliminary Interview

As soon as potential candidates are gathered, the preliminary interviews are started. Preliminary interviews are typically conducted by phone and are next in the filtering process. If the preliminary interview is successful, the hiring probability moves up to around forty-five percent (figure 2-2B).

## 3. Successful In-Person Interview

The next step is the in-person interview(s). This step involves the hiring manager and other key personnel interviews. It may take a few weeks for everyone to interview the candidate. If this step is successful, however, the hiring probability goes up to eighty-five percent (figure 2-2C).

## 4. Reference Check

During the reference check phase, there is a chance that questions may arise about the candidate's background. This may put uncertainty in the mind of the hiring manager and may cause the hiring probability percentage to drop slightly to around seventy-five percent (figure 2-2D).

## 5. Offer

A unique situation occurs when the offer is presented to the candidate. The hiring percentage actually drops significantly to approximately sixty percent (figure 2-2E). There are a number of possible reasons for this:

1. The candidate's current company may make a counteroffer that lures them back. This may include the promotion that the candidate wanted.

85% of surveyed companies said that attracting and retaining the *"Right"* talent was *"Very Important."*

Source: *"Flexibility Moves to Center Stage,"* Workforce Management Magazine, December 2004, p. 86.

2. The candidate may have or be waiting for offers from other companies. The other company(s) may be closer, pay more money, or offer more of a challenge.

3. The candidate may decide not to accept the move once they realize that they will have to make a major career decision.

Therefore, the offer point is the must critical in all of the recruiting steps. It is the pivotal point in the entire recruiting process when everything comes to the final candidate's decision.

### 6. Acceptance or Rejection of Offer

If the candidate accepts the offer, the process is complete at one hundred percent (figure 2-2F). If the candidate rejects the offer, the hiring probability goes to zero percent and another candidate must be placed into the process.

# CHAPTER 3
## *The Job Requisition*

It is important to establish essential policies and procedures in the recruiting area. One of these is the job requisition procedure. Once this policy has been established and the procedure written, it will allow the organization to control growth and help to budget overhead. There is a sample requisition form included in this chapter.

### WHAT IS A JOB REQUISITION?

The job requisition process is one of the key steps in talent balancing. Numerous companies have ignored it as just additional paperwork, but it is important to realize that job requisitions provide the first official and financial commitment to adding personnel to the organization. Not only does it define where this person will work in the organization, how much they will earn, and to whom they will report, but additional considerations such as career path, training, and personal growth must be also factored in for future considerations. This will be the first step in staffing a company with long-term, successful employees. The official job requisition also reduces time and energy lost by working on pending job requisitions that may never become real.

## WHY ARE JOB REQUISITIONS IMPORTANT?

The job requisition process allows the company to control staffing costs and corporate growth. When a job requisition is approved by management, a corporate and financial commitment has been made. It is the official document that allows HR to allocate time and budget to the recruiting effort. It also creates the first step in the talent balancing process. This is the time to evaluate what the company needs. When a company authorizes bringing on a full-time employee, it should also investigate the present and future use of the employee. If it appears that the company will not use the employee after three to nine months, it will probably be better to bring in a consultant or temporary employee. This investigation also determines what the actual cost of having that full-time employee is. Wages are just a part of employee costs. There are also the cost to hire, insurance and other employee benefits computer, furniture, office space, office supplies, and so on.

## THE EIGHT-STEP JOB REQUISITION PROCEDURE

1. Evaluate the need
2. Create the job requisition
3. Authorize the job requisition
4. Approve the job requisition
5. Open the requisition
6. Perform the search or change the requisition
7. Close the requisition
8. Create pending requisitions

### Step 1: Evaluate the Need

The first step in the job requisition procedure is to evaluate the need for a full-time employee. It must be determined if there is enough work for this position to be full-time. The alternatives are to decide if it should be part-time or should be taken care of by an outside consultant. This is an important step because you do not want to hire staff that you cannot afford or that is not needed, or is not needed at this time. Asking the current staff about the workload will give you insight into what may be needed, both now and in the future. Make sure that you figure in a two-month lead time to do the recruiting.

## *Step 2: Create the Job Requisition (Originator)*

The originator begins the process by creating s job requisition and submitting it to the authorizer for approval. This can be done either on-line or manually depending on the system in place in your company. A standard job requisition includes the following information (see Form 3-1):

### *Job Requisition Form Detailed Information*

- Job requisition number—unique number for each job requisition, usually sequential
- Type of requisition—new, replacement, or substantially changed. "New job/position" or "substantially changed" status must be reviewed by compensation before posting
- Department—name and department accounting number
- Reporting supervisor—name, title, and department of the position's supervisor
- Location—the location(s) of the openings
- Job title—new or established job title
- Number needed—number of openings for this requisition
- Special background check required?—verify if high security or special background check needed
- Reason for requisition
- Budget—is this requisition budgeted or not?
- For job/position vacated, provide name of person being replaced
- Created by—person initiating requisition
- Authorized by—person in your department designated with the authority to approve this level of requisition
- Job requirements—attach approved job description or create new one; designate both "required" and "desired"
- Responsibilities—duties of the position
- Experience—list years and type of experience
- Education—indicate required degrees and majors
- Location—indicate the location where the position is to reside
- Telecommute?—yes or no
- US citizen required?—yes or no
- Work Visa acceptable?—yes or no
- Full-time, temporary, or part-time—indicate hiring status; if temporary or part-time, indicate start date and end date
- Desired start date—Insert date or indicate if position recruitment tied to sales or other conditions (e.g., must be hired after department manager)

- Indicate shift—first, second, or third
- Travel required?—indicate percent
- Internal post?—if yes, indicate posting duration in days (typically fourteen days)
- Salary—indicate a range, along with any bonuses, commissions, or benefits
- Salary grade
- Employment grade
- Relocation allocation?—if so, indicate budgetary number
- requisition filled—name(s) of new employee(s)
- Start date(s) of new employee(s)

### Step 3: Authorize the Job Requisition (Authorizer)

When the originator submits the completed requisition, the authorizer reviews it as necessary, and approves or denies it. The authorizer may accept the requisition contingent on sales or other variables. The originator is then notified of the authorizer's action. If the authorizer approves the requisition, it is sent to HR, and the recruiting process is officially started. If the authorizer denies the requisition, it is so noted, copies are sent to the originator and HR, and the process ends. A denied requisition can be viewed but not acted upon.

### Step 4: Approve the Job Requisition

Once it has been approved, HR reviews the job posting to verify that it meets all parameters. If the position is new or substantially changed, HR must fill in the required information such as compensation, reporting structure, and/or overlapping job requirements. When all review is complete, HR approves the requisition, and, if so designated, internal postings are distributed (physically or electronically) to selected location(s). The originator is notified of the approval and HR moves into the next step.

### Step 5: Open the Requisition

Once HR has approved the job requisition, the search can be formally started. A status report is created that lists all of the open requisitions, pending requisitions, and status of each. This can be reviewed by the senior staff or hiring managers at the weekly status meetings. Some companies put the status report online for easy access and update.

### Step 6: Perform the Search or Change the Requisition

The recruiter(s) begin the actual search based on the job requisition, noting that the requisition could change after the first few interviews. If there are any major changes to the requisition during the search process, it must go back through the approval process once again. It may be determined that the salary range was too low when the job requisition was first created. When the new job requisition is approved, it will be necessary to meet with the hiring manager and develop a new job description before starting the search.

---

### Case Example 3-1: Modify the Requisition

*A company needs a senior MIS analyst for its small MIS department. After interviewing a few candidates, listening to the types of questions they were asking, and hearing what these applicants felt was needed, it was decided that they really needed an MIS manager. It was obvious that they did not need another analyst, but more of an architect who could plan for future growth. The job requisition needed to be updated to a manager level, with different salary, job description, and reporting structure. In this situation, the hiring process revealed a problem that management did not know that they had.*

---

### Step 7: Close the Requisition

The job requisition can be closed in one of two ways. The first is that after the candidate has been hired, the requisition is closed by filling in the name of the new employee, the start date, and salary, and forwarding it to HR. If the employee does not make it through the probationary period, the requisition can be reused as is (unless major changes are made). The second reason to close a requisition is because the company has put a freeze on hiring, or it has been determined that the position is no longer needed or no longer affordable. Job requisitions can be put on hold also.

### Step 8: Create Pending Job Requisitions

When a company starts budgeting for staffing, they usually start with a list of pending job requisitions. This list usually contains all of the possible hires, departments, and titles. Most companies do not go into further detail until they are converted into official job requisitions. If this list is used properly, it can be used to look ahead at what recruiting activities will be coming in the future. The successful recruiter uses this pending job list to keep an eye out for those special candidates that they may run across while recruiting for other approved positions. In the process of running references or sourcing, recruiters usually run into a number of related people who are, at the time, looking for new employment. Finding really good people takes a lot of work and no one wants to pass up superstars. In some situations, it may be better to hire a superstar a little early in the schedule than to lose them. Sometimes it is desirable to keep in constant communication with them until the requisition is opened.

## Form 3-1

## JOB REQUISITION FORM

Requisition #_____

| I. POSITION INFORMATION (to be completed by Hiring Manager) |
|---|

| Job Title: | Hiring Manager: |

| Salary Grade: | Salary Range: MIN _____ MID _____ MAX _____ |

| Date Needed: | Department: | Location: | ☐ Exempt ☐ Non-Exempt |

| ☐ Regular ☐ Full-Time<br>☐ Temporary ☐ Part-Time | Hours/Days: | Length of Assignment:<br>From: _____ To: _____ |

| Budgeted? ☐ Yes<br>☐ No Approval_____ | Does a current employee qualify? ☐ Yes ☐ No<br>If Yes, please give employee's name: |

| If not budgeted, give reason: _____ | If replacement, for whom?: _____<br>Replaced Person: ☐ Promoted ☐ Transferred<br>☐ Terminated ☐ Other |
| Work space allocated? ☐ Yes ☐ No<br>Equipment ordered? ☐ Phone ☐ Computer ☐ Cell ☐ PDA<br>Other: _____ | Change date: _____<br>Explain: _____ |

| Knowledge, Skills, Abilities Required: _____ | Education, Experience Needed: _____ |

| Comments: _____ | Comments: _____ |

| II. RECRUITING PLAN (to be completed by Hiring Manager & Human Resources Department) |
|---|

| 1. INTERVIEW PROCESS |
|---|

| Preferred Interview Days/Dates: |

| 1st Interview: | 2nd Interview: | Final: |
|---|---|---|
| | | |
| | | Other |

*(continued)*

## Form 3-1
*Continued*

| 2. SOURCING/ADVERTISING |
|---|

**2a. Sourcing**

| | | |
|---|---|---|
| ❏ Agency/Retained/Contract Recruiter | ❏ | Colleges/Universities |
| ❏ Internet Services | ❏ | Internal Candidates |
| ❏ Open House | ❏ | EDD |
| ❏ Job Fair | ❏ | Suggested Leads |
| ❏ Professional Associations/Organizations | ❏ | Employee Referral |

**2b. Advertising**

Where/Publication:

| Dates: | Estimated Cost: |
|---|---|

Comments/Recommendations: _____

| 3. ACTION STEPS |
|---|

❏   Create Recruiting Plan


Review progress on: _____

| **III. HIRING INFORMATION** (to be completed by Human Resources Department) | |
|---|---|
| Date Requisition Opened: | Date Requisition Closed: |
| Person Hired: (First, Middle Initial, Last): | Start Date: |

| **IV. APPROVALS** (all signatures required) | | | |
|---|---|---|---|
| Supervisor: | Date: | Next Level Review: | Date: |
| Second Level Review: | Date: | Human Resources: | Date: |

# CHAPTER 4
## Managing the Hiring Managers

*Hiring manager* is the term given to anyone to whom the new employee will report directly. They don't even have to be a manager; they can be a supervisor, director, or vice president. It is just a term to denote the focal point for the hiring process, and they should be the focal point for the interview cycle as well.

The recruiter's real customer is the hiring manager. The successful recruiter must know exactly what the hiring manager is looking for in a candidate. Even if the recruiter has a good job description, the hiring manager must be interviewed to determine any attributes that cannot be easily written down or are missing. It is vital to determine the hiring manager's likes, dislikes, and expectations. The successful recruiter must be able to form a close relationship with the hiring manager in order to fill the position. In this chapter, we discuss some of the important steps in how to manage the hiring manager.

### CREATE A JOINT OWNERSHIP OF THE PROJECT WITH THE HIRING MANAGER

The hiring manager must think of the recruiting process as a joint ownership project with the recruiter. The recruiter is expected to bring in qualified candidates and the hiring manager is expected to respond in a timely manner. It is essential that the recruiter is informed as soon as possible if the resumes are or are not acceptable." In addition, the hiring manager must report back to the recruiter in a timely manner so the process continues to move forward. The staffing project must be jointly owned in order to make it work.

## INTERVIEWING THE HIRING MANAGER

The basics of a successful staffing program and the best way to bring talent balancing to your organization is to determine exactly what is needed by the hiring manager. This will be the foundation for the job description. An accurate job description is essential in the staffing process. The recruiter's fundamental activity is to determine, "What does the hiring manager really want?" Start the process by asking the hiring manager to define the position in their own terms. Find out what happened to past employees who were in this position. What were their good and bad points? In addition to the written job description, it is important to determine the best type of personality that will fit into the corporate culture. What kind of personality do they work with best? Ask the hiring manager, "What are the three most important characteristics of the job?" These will be your key criteria in the recruiting process. In addition, ask for some key words that describe the position that can be used in Internet searching. Ask the hiring manager where they would look if they were doing the search—what companies, competitors, vendors, or associations, or is there anyone that they know who could do the job. Be sure to find out if there are any companies where you should not recruit. The hiring manager may have some joint ventures with companies that should not be raided by the recruiter.

Interview other people in the same department who may hold similar positions and get a feel from them about how they perceive the job and what is important to them. Also, ask them if they know anyone who would be a possible candidate. Even if they just have a name and do not know a way of contacting the person, you may be able to track them down on the Internet. The key questions to ask each hiring manager are listed in Form 4-1 at the end of this chapter.

Every hiring manager has a preferred method of interviewing. The successful recruiter will find out their process and work with the hiring manager. Some managers will want to do phone interviews first and some may only want to do in-person interviews. Some may want to see at least three or four candidates before they make a decision. The hiring manager typically will want other staff members to assist in the interview process. Some will want to do group interviews and some will want to do individual interviews. Everyone has their own style and it is the responsibility of the successful recruiter to identify and follow it.

## THE HIRING MANAGER AND RECRUITER RELATIONSHIP

After the meeting with the hiring manager, the recruiter must create a job description based on the information gathered and start the search. The recruiter should do a preliminary interview with any potential candidates to determine the interest level, compensation requirements, and verify that he meets the minimum job requirements. This process will save the hiring managers valuable time.

The first few acceptable resumes that the recruiter sends to the hiring manager are termed "calibration resumes," because they are designed to find out if the search is on the right track. The search may have to start all over if there is any misinformation or data missing from the job description or if changes have been made after the interview process. This is a common problem on the part of some hiring managers because they may not be really sure what they want until they review a few resumes. So it is important that the recruiter get feedback as soon as possible to make sure they are on the right track. Once that is confirmed, the recruiter can start "filling up the pipeline" with candidates.

Some of the people that will be found fall into the category of passive candidates, which simply means that they are not actively looking for a job. They may not even have an up-to-date resume until you get them to write one. Once these people have updated their resumes, they get interested in the job search process and they will start sending their resumes to other companies. Because of this and the fact that good people get hired quickly, it is essential that the hiring manager give a rapid response on resumes that are sent to them. It is important to let the recruiter know as soon as possible the following:

1. Does the hiring manager want to interview the candidate?
2. What was the problem with the resume? What experience was missing? Does the job description need to be changed or updated?

If the job description needs to be changed, the recruiting process may be delayed. If it is changed too much from the original, the search may have to be restarted from the beginning. This may happen more than one would like to think.

Once the interview process has been completed, the recruiter needs to know the interest level as soon as possible also. If the recruiter has done their job properly, the candidates will have the proper background, salary level, and experience and the interview process will reveal if there is the right chemistry between the hiring manager and the prospect. In addition the recruiter needs to know if the interview process has modified any of the job parameters as soon as possible. A decision needs to be made by the hiring manager whether the candidate needs to continue to the next step, just be kept "warm," or can be released with a reject letter. Remember, these candidates now have their resumes on the market and are usually talking to other companies. If they are ignored or there is too much of a delay getting them through the interview and offer process, they may be lost. Knowing this, the offer process must also move quickly. If the interviews have gone well, it is important to know the official company posture on salary range, perks, and benefits for the job in question. These parameters are typically defined in the job requisition process when the job is first opened, but if not, they must be established as soon as possible so a correct, viable offer can be made.

Decisions on the "offer" parameters must be verified so that paperwork can be expedited through HR in order to get a written job offer into the hands of the candidate as soon as possible. Remember, you may be one of many companies that will be making written job offers. Looking decisive and professional will go a long way in influencing the candidate. They must be kept feeling wanted until the offer is made or they will go elsewhere. This can only be done for a short period of time, however.

Most hiring managers will want to make a verbal offer to the candidate before the formal offer letter goes out. If the recruiter has done the job, there should be no surprises in what the candidate wants, and they should accept. After the candidate has returned the signed offer letter, it is essential that either the hiring manager or recruiter continue to contact the candidate a couple of times a week until they show up for their first day of work. This professional activity will keep the candidate feeling that they made the right decision.

It also helps prevent other companies from stealing your candidate away before they even start.


## POTENTIAL PROBLEMS WITH THE HIRING MANAGER

The successful recruiter must be aware that the hiring manager may have a number of unseen shortcomings. One problem is that they really do not know all the job talents needed. That is why it is important to tell them that the first resumes you are going to send them are Calibration Resumes. These will be resumes that appear to be close to the job description and can give the hiring manager the direction in which the recruiter is going. If the hiring manager rejects these resumes, it is time to have another meeting to review and update the job description because something has changed. Before the meeting, highlight the key attributes in each resume and discuss each one with the hiring manager.

If, after interviewing a few candidates, the hiring manager does not like any of the candidates you have provided, you may be the victim of the "creeping job description." This can occur when the hiring manager is slowly realizing that there are different or new job requirements needed for the position. The experience level or background may also be slowly changing. The hiring manager may have brought in another person who has some of the experience necessary in the position that is still open.

The hiring manager who works with the recruiter and gives timely, accurate feedback will usually find the staff they need in a timely manner. Other hiring managers may have shortcomings or hidden agendas that the recruiter is unaware of.


### The Hiring Manager Who Does Not Like to Interview

Some managers (especially in the technical sciences) really do not like to interview. In order to solve this problem, it may be necessary to have one of their senior staff do the initial interview. If they think the candidate is good, they can include the hiring manager in the next interview round. Another method is to suggest a group interview process. Having their staff help interview will make it easier on reluctant hiring managers. Other problems include:

1. The hiring manager is too "busy" to interview
2. The hiring manager is waiting for the "perfect" candidate
3. The hiring manager has a hidden agenda

---

### Case Example 4-1: Hiring Manager with a Hidden Agenda

*A professional, proactive recruiter was working with a hiring manager at a satellite communication company on the West Coast. The recruiter continued to present resumes of outstanding candidates and was continually ignored and put off by the hiring manager. It appeared that the hiring manager had some type of hidden agenda, so the frustrated recruiter finally went to management to see if they had any advice. She learned that the hiring manager was consistently missing deadlines and was using the lack of staff problem as his excuse. When pressed by management, he finally admitted that he was in over is head, did not know how to do the project, and was using the staffing problem excuse until he could find a new job. He never planned to interview or hire anyone at any time. He soon left the company and it only took the new manager a few weeks to hire for the opening.*

---

### Case Example 4-2: Hiring Manager with Discrimination

*An order processing department needed five people to work on the new contract. The recruiter started the search and started to find qualified people almost immediately. As she sent the resumes to the hiring managers, she was very confused by the number being sent back marked "no interest." The recruiter took the job description and resumes to the senior recruiter to see what she was doing wrong. The senior recruiter noticed that the only acceptable resumes had Asian names. The other recruiter replied that the hiring manager was a middle-aged Asian woman. The two recruiters decided to do an experiment. They took one of the early rejected resumes and changed the name to an Asian sounding name and re-submitted it. They made no changes to the resume content. Almost immediately the hiring manager requested to do a phone interview with the phony candidate. The discrimination problem was reported to HR management and they dealt with the problem.*

---

The best way to work with the "problem" hiring manager is to go to their boss and ask for assistance. The problem may be solved simply by the boss asking the hiring manager to be more responsive to the recruiting effort.

## HIRING MANAGER COMMUNICATIONS

The key to a good relationship with the hiring manager is good communication. Most hiring managers are very busy and may not give recruiting the time that it needs. If you are having trouble getting time with the hiring manager, you might want to try to meet during breakfast, lunch, or dinner, or after hours. The key is to show them that the process will work only if they are part of it. Three simple steps are needed from the hiring manager. Step one is to provide a fast response and analysis on resumes submitted by the recruiter. Step two is to work closely with the recruiter during the interview process. Step three is to be available for the offer process when it comes up. The hiring manager who is most reactive will end up with the best people. The hiring manager who is too busy to bother with recruiting will either never get staffed up or end up with inferior talent.

---

### Case Example 4-3: The Young Hiring Manager

*The young hiring manager really needed to hire a new warehouse manager as soon as possible. The recruiter assigned to the search had come up with a few people who really looked good and passed the initial phone call interview. After several e-mails that were unanswered by the hiring manager, the recruiter took the resumes to the hiring manager's office and was discussing them when the president came. The president looked at the resumes and said to the hiring manager, "This person really looks good. Interview him when you come back from your trip." When he got back, the recruiter went to him to schedule the interview. "Oh, I met a person on the plane that knew the candidate and he said he was no good." The recruiter asked who he was, and where they had worked together. The hiring manager did not know. The recruiter asked what was said about the candidate and when did it happen. The hiring manager said he could not remember. The recruiter went to the president with the story. The president told the recruiter to send all the candidates to one of the Board members for first interviews. The Board member found a good candidate. He would take him to the hiring manager and they would interview the applicant together. After a while, the new hiring manager learned how to interview and the selection was made.*

---

## SUMMARY

The recruiting process is a joint partnership between recruiters and hiring managers. If either party does not take responsibility and act quickly, the position(s) will not be filled, and good people will be lost. The professional recruiter will drive the process and make sure that the goals are met. Communication is key in this process. The recruiter must make sure that communication between the candidates and hiring manager are accurate and timely. There should never be a time when no one knows what is going on. The professional hiring manager must make sure that the candidate who is hired is the best of the group that was interviewed and that it is the person that *they* want. They should not hire just to fill the opening. The hiring manager must feel that the person has the capability to do a good job and can be moved through the organization effectively. These hires should be made from a position of strength and not fear. If the recruiter can manage the hiring manager, bring them qualified candidates, maintain accurate communications, and keep them on schedule, the team will be successful and the company will have a talented staff.

**Form 4-1**
**Hiring Manager Interview Checklist**

Hiring Manager Name:_____

Contact: Phone_____Email_____

**Positions Responsible and Priority:**

Position                    Priority

_____

_____

_____

_____

**Interview Preference**

☐ Yes  ☐ No  ☐ NA    Initial Phone Interview

☐ Yes  ☐ No  ☐ NA    Group Interviews

☐ Yes  ☐ No  ☐ NA    Staff Interview

**Hiring Manager Questions:**

☐ What is *your* definition of the job?

☐ Do you agree with the compensation package for this position?

☐ What educational background do you want?

☐ Are there any special credentials or certifications needed?

☐ How many years of experience does this position need?

☐ What type of personality will fit your opening?

☐ Do you have any personalities that are difficult to get along with?

☐ What are some of the key words for this industry and this position?

☐ What are the "must-haves" and the "would-like-to-haves"?

☐ What are the *top three attributes* that are mandatory for this position?

☐ What will this person do for the first three to six months that they are here?

☐ Do *you* know anyone who can do the job?

☐ In what companies/competitors/vendors can we find a person like this?

☐ Are there any companies that you have strategic alliances with that we should not recruit?

☐ If there is anyone in the group that is a close fit to this position, we would like to talk to them.

☐ How have you found people in the past?

☐ Have you interviewed a lot of people?

☐ What worked and what did not work in recruiting for this position?

☐ Who was the last person that rejected your offer for this position?

☐ What happened to the last person in this position?

☐ Do you like to make verbal offers yourself, or do you have anyone else do it?

# CHAPTER 5
## Job Descriptions and Salary Structures

### THE IMPORTANCE OF THE JOB DESCRIPTION

The importance of a well-written job description consists of more than a list of responsibilities that the job entails. It should reflect corporate culture and the priorities of the organization. Job descriptions provide an opportunity to clearly communicate your company direction and where the employee fits in the big picture. It is also an opportunity for management to use the talent balancing techniques to find and retain the "superstars." Writing job descriptions allows the hiring manager to sit down and mentally build their organization with an eye on work activities now and in the future. Proper time and effort must be given to the creation of the job description. The hiring manager can also determine their department's weaknesses and use the new job description to shore up the talent needed.

Whether you're a small business or a large, multisite organization, well-written job descriptions will help you define employee direction and capabilities. Alignment of the people you employ with your goals, vision, and mission will result in success for your organization. As a leader, you must assure the job description is valid for today and into the future, and hire the strongest talent available. You do not want to bring in people who are needed now but not later. This is a critical step in the talent balancing philosophy.

Most HR job descriptions only cover legal matters such as "must be able to carry fifty pounds," "must have a valid driver's license," and so on. Some hiring managers will have detailed job descriptions, but, as time passes, projects change and the corporate needs change. Therefore, it is imperative that the hiring manager, some of their staff, and HR meet to determine what is really needed. The result should be a concise, up-to-date, and detailed job description. The job description can be compared to a blueprint or specification. It is the foundation of the search and without the proper job description, the correct talent may not be hired.

You can also think of job descriptions as communication tools for your organization. Candidates want to know exactly what you are looking for in the position and what is expected of them. I know some hiring managers who have scared off candidates that they knew could not do the job. Management and the rest the organization should be aware of the job description so they know the direction in which the department is going. In start-ups, where the organizational chart is often highly fluid, job descriptions can be particularly valuable because they help managers understand how the organization is evolving, and this knowledge allow them to reassign people and redefine roles to help achieve the company's long-term goals.

The job description is the blueprint or specification necessary for the search. If the job description is incorrect, everyone will be wasting his or her time and the incorrect people may be hired. Having written job descriptions for every employee also establishes clear expectations about who does what. That way, when somebody steps outside of his or her role, others will be able to acknowledge it. If the responsibilities change, the job description should be updated by the employee or their hiring manager. This also helps the hiring manager be aware of burnout or ending up with the talent base being unbalanced. New jobs may need to be created to balance the workload. In a start-up or rapidly growing organization, it's common for people to take on more than they can handle. Tracking their responsibilities can help hiring managers deploy their most valuable people more effectively, and get help when responsibilities grow too many for one person to handle alone. In addition, developing job descriptions is an excellent way to involve people in your organization in making talent balancing a success.

Job descriptions set clear expectations for what you expect from the employees. This will assist during performance reviews and work flow analysis. If the job description is too vague, it will be difficult to determine if the employee is doing what needs to be done. Without the guidance of detailed job descriptions, employees will have a tendency to do the things that they like to do and may ignore the tough tasks that really need to be addressed in a timely manner. This is especially important for new positions that have not had the luxury of previous incumbents to assist in the job analysis.

Maintaining and updating job descriptions as time goes on is also important. Doing so helps you follow where people start and how they develop over a period of time. There may be some positions that evolve into totally different acts of responsibilities after a period of time. By updating the job description during every performance review, you can assist the employee in defining higher goals and objectives. This will also assist management in evaluating all of their talent and in balancing the work with the capability. It will also keep you informed when roles change in your organization. When you know this, you can open a dialogue with the employees who may or may not like the new roles they find themselves in. It will give you a good opportunity to find out if you may lose a good but unhappy employee. You must keep your finger on this pulse to continue your talent balancing.

---

### Case Example 5-1: The Short Job Description

*The hiring manager said he knew exactly what he wanted: a controller with five to seven years of experience with a public company, who made sure the financial statements were accurate and on time, and who worked well under pressure. It was a very short job description based on a three-minute phone call. The recruiter started the search and, after a while, came up with three resumes that met the terse job description. He sent them to the hiring manager who immediately wanted to start interviewing. After the third interview, the hiring manager was furious. "None of these people have Sarbanes-Oxley experience!" he yelled. The recruiter picked up the job description and said, "That's not in the job description!" The hiring manager replied, "Well, I thought you would just know that. It is the most important attribute!" The recruiter rewrote the job description and started the search from scratch; valuable time had been lost because of an incomplete job description and lack of communication.*

---

## BASICS OF THE CREATION OF A JOB DESCRIPTION

1. Determine the job title. Human Resources typically has established job titles on file and pay ranges related to each level.

If the job is new, however, the hiring manager, HR, and management should be responsible for establishing the exact job title and salary range. Job titles should be similar to other comparable industrial positions. If you make it too unique no one will be able to recognize it and recruiting will be difficult. Some titles can even work against you. Aim for something realistic that reflects what the worker actually does and pay attention to the tasks at hand. Another point to consider is that some international companies only want to work with vice presidents or directors level people. In addition, avoid ambiguous or inconsistent titles that will end up just confusing people. After the major functions have been identified, verify that the job title still matches the responsibilities (see step 2).

2. Establish the major functions. List all of the major job functions for this position. Be sure to include any other activities that this position may support or fill in for on a part-time basis. Include any reporting responsibilities the position will have and what the level of management or customer contact there will be with this position. Establish the top three attributes that this position must have in order to perform the job. Also, outline the career growth progression for the successful employee.

3. Establish the percentage of these functions in relation to the total job. For each function, determine the duties or actions undertaken when performing the job satisfactorily. In addition, establish the frequency of each duty (i.e., daily, weekly, monthly).

4. Determine the requirements of the position, including skills, knowledge, and abilities needed. The skills, knowledge, and abilities should be tied directly to the duties (actions) to be performed in the job. A knowledge or skill is something you know or can do that helps you perform the duties of your job well, such as public speaking skills or negotiation expertise.

5. Establish the number of years of experience necessary along with past job titles held for this position.

6. Determine the location of the position, and estimate the amount of travel required (expressed as a percentage).

7. Establish the level and type of college degrees, certifications, or credentials necessary.

8. Determine total compensation package (and related costs for this position), consisting of the salary range, standard corporate benefits, bonuses, special benefits, vacation, sign-on bonus, flex benefits, stock or stock options, relocation fees, and contingency or retained search fees,

9. Write the summary statement, providing a brief job overview. Determine the degree of supervision and include this in the summary if applicable.

10. Add all federal and state requirements for the Equal Employment Opportunity Commission (EEO) or the Americans with Disabilities Act (ADA) that are required by law. Warning! A job description is generally regarded as a legal document. Any reference to race, color, religion, age, sex, national origin or nationality, or physical or mental disability is illegal.

11. Verify term of employment. Is this position part time or full time? Will the length of employment be tied of any type of contract? This information should be established when the job description is approved.

12. Create a brief outline of the goals or activities for this position for the first six months after hiring.

13. Write a short two or three paragraph job description (including the hiring manager's input) to be used by the recruiters and HR staff.

14. Establish the corporate level for this position in order to determine the size of the office, type of furniture, PDA, corporate credit card, corporate car, cell phone, notebook computer, and so on. If the employee will work from home, determine the office tools that will be provided by the company, such as a separate phone line, fax, fast internet line, furniture, and the like.

## HIDDEN JOB DESCRIPTION INFORMATION

The most difficult part of the job description is establishing just exactly what the person will be doing and how they will interface with the rest of the organization. The HR department may have an outdated or inaccurate job description. In order to find the best candidate for the opening, a thorough job description must be created. It will be necessary to interview the hiring manager, and if possible, the incumbent in order to create a true and accurate job description. Have the hiring manager and incumbent (if available) meet and ask them to do the following:

1. Spend some time thinking about the job. Make notes, or keep a diary of work-related activities.
2. Determine if there are other responsibilities that should be under this position. *Note:* Focus on the facts. Do not overstate or understate duties, knowledge, skills, abilities, and other characteristics. Refrain from side issues. This activity is only concerned with the job itself. Job performance, wages, complaints, relationships with coworkers, and the like are not relevant to this activity.
3. Validate the job descriptions and salary range with other positions in the department and industry.
4. Determine what the other perks are for this position such as bonuses, sign-on bonus, stock or stock options, promotional rewards, or some form of flex benefits.
5. Establish if there are other responsibilities that are being handled elsewhere that should be under this position.
6. Verify that one person can handle all of the responsibilities of this position. It may be necessary to hire an assistant or cut back on the tasks to make the work able to be done.

---

*Case Example 5-2: Working Around a Job Description*

*The software certification manager was approached by a young technician who tested power supplies on the production line. He was about to graduate with honors, with a degree in computer science, and was anxious to get into his first love, software programming field. The manager created a job description for a new position called Jr. Programmer, grade level of 35, and submitted it to HR. The HR manager immediately rejected it, indicating that the applicant was currently at grade level 36 and although the pay level was the same, policy would not allow anyone to transfer into a lower grade level. The hiring manager waited thirty days then rewrote the job description with a new title of Associate Software Certifier, grade level 36 (same salary as before). HR passed it right through, the applicant transferred, and became one of the best young superstars in the department. Moral of the story: Don't let a job description keep you from getting good people!*

---

## SALARY STRUCTURES AND COMPENSATION PROGRAMS

If the department has not hired anyone in a few years, they may experience salary "sticker shock," when they find out what the industry is now paying for their positions. If your company is out of sync with the rest of the industry, you now have a problem called "salary compression." This may result in hiring new people from the outside who make twenty percent more than your top performer with similar experience.

It is fairly easy to see what your competitors are paying for similar positions by looking at job boards on the Internet or talking to HR associations such as The Society of Human Resource Management (SHRM) or Professionals in Human Resources Association (PIHRA).

Salary compression occurs when there are shortages of key positions in the industry and their related salary increases. While this is going on outside your top performer continues to receive the corporate approved three percent salary increase per year. It will be tough to find someone who is making below the industry salary level to take your job. As soon as they get an offer from a competitor paying a competitive salary, they will be gone.

The real answer is to bring your staff salaries up to the industry standard. In order to do this, you must implement a "fast track salary implementation program." Instead of giving them all of the money up front, you ramp it up every six months until you have met the industry average. This action may prevent some of your current staff from leaving to seek higher wages elsewhere. Putting those on the fast track will allow the experienced, loyal, top performer(s) to be at the same salary level as the new hire.

If, for some reason, you cannot afford to increase your employees' salary, provide them with other perks such as:

- An aggressive profit-sharing program
- Added vacation
- Every other Friday off during summer
- Special private parking space
- Liberal expense account
- Special insurance program
- Special bonus program

There are a number of inexpensive methods you can use to help keep those key employees such as a bigger office, better furniture, or newer computer.

## SUMMARY

Job descriptions are written statements that describe the duties, responsibilities, required qualifications, reporting relationships, compensation package, experience, and schooling for all jobs in your organization. This information is gathered based on objective information obtained through job analysis, an understanding of the competencies and skills required to accomplish needed tasks, and how the individual will fit within the organization. Job descriptions clearly identify and spell out the responsibilities of a specific job so there is no question about what the worker will be doing.

Well-written and clear-cut job descriptions can help you select your preferred candidates and address the issues and questions of those people who were not selected. Well-written job descriptions help the employees who must work with the person hired to understand the boundaries of the new person's responsibilities.

Job descriptions can be the foundation for an orchestrated recruiting, development, and retention strategy that are the basics of the talent balancing philosophy. Establishing clear objectives from the beginning, updating job descriptions as people take on more work, and regularly discussing the employees' job satisfaction will assist you in creating and maintaining an effective workforce for your organization.

**Form 5-1**
**Job Description Checklist**

- ❐ Hiring manager name
- ❐ Date required
- ❐ Determine job title
- ❐ Establish the major functions
- ❐ Determine the requirements of the position
- ❐ Establish the number of years of experience
- ❐ Determine the location of the position
- ❐ Estimate the amount of travel
- ❐ Verify education, certifications, or credentials necessary
- ❐ Determine total compensation package
- ❐ Verify term of employment
- ❐ Determine the top three attributes for this position
- ❐ Create goals or activities for first six months

# CHAPTER 6
## *The Search*

The most difficult recruiting step is doing the actual search. There are many ways to find talent but there is no "sure-fire" method that works every time. The recruiter has to look at these processes like a carpenter looks at a toolbox. Every search will use different tools. A search plan must be created and the recruiting tools should be selected at that time.

### CREATING THE SEARCH PLAN

The recruiter must create a search plan that will be based on the budget, time frame, and types of positions. The budget is usually based on how fast the talent must be hired, how difficult the search, and the number of openings. In some searches, the candidates must have very specialized skills and are difficult to find. You may have to go to a costly outside "boutique contingency search firm" that is dedicated to a very small, specialized segment of the workforce. Advertising and job fairs can be costly also, but if you have a large number of open requisitions, taking a half-page ad and advertising for all the openings may be cost effective. These are just a few things to consider when you are creating the search plan. When you are creating the plan, it is important to talk to HR and the hiring managers to identify what worked (and did not work) in the past. For example, if the company always

| Best Hiring Sources | |
| --- | --- |
| Internet/Database | 56.0% |
| Employee Referral | 12.4% |
| Contract Recruiting, Other | 10.0% |
| Retained | 4.7% |
| Organizational Sites | 4.3% |
| Print | 3.8% |
| Direct | 3.3% |
| Events | 2.8% |
| Contingency Search | 2.7% |

Source: "Soft Markets for the Long Term," *Workforce Management Magazine*, December 2004, p. 98.

goes to job fairs but never seems to hire anyone, there is no reason to add this to your search plan.

The search plan also needs to establish the hiring priorities. Typically, if you are hiring a department manager and staff to work for them, you want to hire the manager first, so that the manager will have a hand in building their own group. This will ensure a strong group so long as the manager is the right caliber and the recruiter is doing their job properly.

The time frame will come from the business plan and budget. The customer service staff may not be ready to be hired until the sales staff is on board and generating revenue. Estimating when an employee is going to be hired is difficult at best. Recruiters never know when they will find those qualified candidates. It may be the first person they talk to or the one hundredth; there is no easy way to predict which it will be. The search plan is so important because all the recruiting techniques can be reviewed and the ones that appear to have the best chance of working are chosen. Once the plan has been approved, it must be closely followed. If, after a couple of months, it appears that the plan must be modified because time goals are not being met, make the changes quickly and get back to working the modified plan. If things are not working, *change!* The corporation does not have time to work plans that are not effective.

## RECRUITING TOOLS

Listed below are most of the recruiting tools being used today. With the Internet and specialized programs, new methods are being presented everyday, but the methods in the list below are all proven to work and will bring in qualified candidates. They are not in any particular order, and it should be noted that some will work and some will not for your organization. Please consider all of these tools for your own search plan.

## *Advertising*

Newspaper and magazine advertising costs can vary from hundreds of dollars to tens of thousand of dollars, depending on where and when the ad is placed. Once again, your budget may dictate whether or not you will be doing this type of advertising. If you do advertise, you must evaluate the printing time frame also. Most newspapers can run ads in a few days; magazine advertising, however, will take three to four months' lead time. If you are continually looking for a number of very specialized positions, ongoing, industry-specific magazine advertising campaigns may yield good results. If you have a large number of positions to fill, you may want to consider taking out a half- or full-page newspaper ad. This allows you to advertise all your openings at once as well as having room for a couple of paragraphs about the company, its background, and corporate direction. If you decide to do newspaper advertising, make sure you pick papers servicing the area near your location. Also, do not advertise on holiday weekends. Studies show that people do not read the classifieds on weeks that have a holiday. Some papers will run special employment issues several times a year. These are good opportunities to get good visibility and should be seriously considered.

## *HR Resumes*

Your company will be getting resumes e-mailed and snail mailed to them on an ongoing basis. Hopefully, HR has been doing its job and keeping them available for review. Some of these people may be off the market, but this is a good place to quickly start your search. When you contact these people you will find that some of them have already taken a job but do not like the company or what they are now doing. They will be more than willing to talk to you about an opening. If you contact them and they are happy where they are at now, ask them if they know of anyone else who is looking or who would know of anyone available. This form of sourcing can pay off because you have a name of a person who referred you, so the call is not really a cold call and is more readily accepted.

## *Word of Mouth*

Word of mouth is the number one method of finding candidates. You never know when your neighbor might have a brother-in-law who is perfect for that sales position you have been looking to fill for the past six months. Make sure you let everyone know the types of people you are looking for. Contact your marketing department and find out if your company is going to any shows or exhibits. If they are, have a large sign made up listing all your current openings and their location(s). A lot of people will be going to these conventions with copies of their resumes in their breast pockets and just looking for an opportunity. If you know other recruiters or HR professionals, send them an e-mail with the job descriptions attached and ask them to keep an eye out or forward any resumes they may have that fit the positions. Let them know that you will do the same for them. Word of mouth is powerful and should be a part of all search plans.

### Employee Referral Programs

One of the best sources for finding candidates is right under your nose: your own employees. By establishing an in-house employee referral program, you can have your employees recommend their friends and business contacts. Who is a better candidate than someone that your own employees refer? It is best to have some type of reward program attached to the employee referral. Money is always a positive motivator which will help expedite the process. Your employees should be paid to assist in company growth; in the long run it is a cost saver. Make sure that the rules of the employee referral program are sent out to everyone before recruiting begins. Here are some key points to remember:

1. Create a form for employees to fill out that asks for their name, the candidate's name, the position, and include a time stamp box so that HR staff can write in the time and date it was accepted and initial it. This will resolve any conflicts that may come up in the future when two employees claim the same candidate. First come, first wins.
2. Post and distribute the job descriptions internally as soon as the recruiting process starts.
3. If the candidate comes in for an interview, make sure the hiring manager has the name of the employee who made the referral. This will allow the hiring manager to talk to the referring employee and gather additional information on the candidate's experience, work ethic, and personality.
4. Be sure to let employees know if their candidate is not going to make it to the second interview. They should be aware of the

outcome, positive or negative. In addition, they should be thanked for trying.

5. If the candidate is hired, make sure that employees are paid their reward as soon as possible. Make sure that all the other employees know about the hiring and the payment. This will show them that it is possible to make money by just filling out a form.

## New Employee Sourcing

Whenever you bring on new employees, they should be given the list of open requisitions and be told about the employee referral program. They will usually know people from their last job who are tired of the old company and ready for a change. New employees are typically very happy about their new position and salary and want to include their business friends and contacts.

## Internal Corporate Postings

You may also have someone inside the corporation who is qualified for the job. The internal job posting can give instructions to the current employee on how to obtain an interview. The best procedure is to have the employee approach their manager with a verbal request that, once approved, can be carried to HR for discussion. If the employee is qualified, an interview can be scheduled. The only problem with this situation is that, if the employee transfers to the new position, the recruiter will now have to fill the position that the inside employee vacated. The good news is that it may be easier to fill than the original job opening.

## Re-Approaching Candidates Who Rejected an Offer in the Past

This unique method is to re-approach candidates that rejected the company's offers in the recent past. In some situations, three to six months after starting a new job candidates realize that they made a mistake but are too embarrassed to contact their old company. If they *are* interested, most of the work has been done; all that may be needed is a new offer letter. If they are happy where they are, you can always source them for new names.

### Professional and Trade Associations

A quick search of the Internet will reveal that there are specific professional industry associations for all professions. If you are looking for a CFO, you can approach some local chapters of a professional organization and ask to have your job posted on their web site or disseminated to their membership. Most of the nonprofit organizations will not have a problem doing this because part of their membership pitch is to offer job leads. It may be necessary to attend these meeting yourself in order to present the open position(s). Here are just a few Internet sites that may help you find associations in your area.

1. Internet Public Library. http://www.ipl.org/
2. National Council of Nonprofit Associations. http://www.ncna.org/
3. The Directory of Associations is a comprehensive source of information on professional, business, and trade associations. http://www.marketingsource.com/associations/
4. Business Organizations Yahoo! www.yahoo.com/Economy/organizations/Professional

### Patents and Trademarks

If you are looking for those unique engineers, scientists, or programmers, go onto the Internet and look for specific patents in the industry. Most scientific patents have multiple names attached to the patent along with a company name. If the people you locate are not interested they may have some excellent names that they can refer to you.

### Past Employees

Ask HR and the hiring managers if there are any past employees who left on their own who they would like to see come back. Contact these people and ask if they would be interested in coming back to work for your company. Most people feel that once they leave a company, they cannot go back. If they are happy where they are, ask them for the names of anyone who may be interested in the job.

### Job Fairs

If your budget can afford it, job fairs are an excellent method of seeing a lot of people in a short time. Job fairs are typically held in hotels or convention centers, last from a few hours to a full day, and usually provide exhibitors with a ten-foot by ten-foot booth. Some job fairs will have private meeting rooms available for interviews and will even provide free copy service for attendees if they run out of their resumes. If you are planning to do a job fair, make sure you follow these recommendations:

1. Find job fairs that represent your type of industry. You will not be successful if you are a mortgage company and you attend a job fair for aerospace and electronics companies.
2. Bring your hiring managers with you so that they can interview on the spot. Some companies are set up to make verbal offers right at the show. This is a great idea if you are recruiting for those hard-to-find positions. Get them before your competition has a chance.
3. Your booth should look professional and successful. An image of success indicates to the candidate that they will be successful, too.
4. Have large signs with all of your job openings (and locations) around your booth so attendees can see them easily from the middle of the aisle. Some people may pass by your booth if it doesn't offer some idea of the job openings or company's products or services.
5. You will be getting a lot of resumes, so make sure you have a procedure to sort them as you get them, using folders or baskets and sort them as you get them. This will greatly expedite the paperwork process when you get back to the office.
6. Always have at least two people working the booth. You don't want to miss anybody or have them waiting too long to talk to a company representative.
7. Make sure you bring literature with the company's background, products and services, benefits, open job descriptions, application forms, business cards, and Web and e-mail addresses. Giveaway items can attract attention, although they are not a necessity.
8. Also, make sure you have a box of stationery items, including pens, a stapler and staples, note pads, safety pins, clear tape, duct tape, and so on, to support the people working the booth.
9. Have water available for the people working in the booth. You will be talking constantly and in an air-conditioned

environment, which can dry out your throat. (Water, incidentally, makes a great giveaway; you're not the only one who is doing a lot of talking.)

10. During the show, try to talk to everyone who stops by regardless of their backgrounds. Be polite and businesslike. If you act brusquely, your manner could leave a negative impression of your company. Remember that you are representing your company and the public is watching closely.

11. Talk to other companies and HR staff when they are available. You may be able to help each other in recruiting or outplacement. The show is an excellent opportunity to see and hear what the rest of the industry is doing. Take advantage of it.

12. Remember that your competitors at the fair have seen your candidates, too. If you find someone with real potential, do not delay in starting the interview process. If you move too slowly, you could lose a valuable candidate.

13. Do a follow-up analysis a few days after the job fair to determine the exact level of success achieved.

### Competitive Companies' Layoffs

The HR department should always be aware of any competitors who are going through layoffs. Most of these competitive HR departments will gladly send you resumes of the staff that they are downsizing. There was one Southern California company that had an open house on their premises and invited recruiters from all over the area to come and interview the employees they had laid off.

### Corporate Open House

Some companies will use advertising to promote their own corporate open house, typically held on a Saturday. Candidates can apply for a position and get interviewed and not take time from the normal work week. It also allows the hiring company to see a lot of people in a short time. Here are some suggestions for a successful open house:

1. Have a sign and balloons directing the candidates to a large area of your company (maybe a large conference room or cafeteria).

2. Have a table for them to sign in where they can see the openings and apply for the appropriate one.

3. Give them an application form, corporate brochures, literature, giveaways, and direct them to the waiting room.
4. Make sure to have drinks and something to eat (doughnuts, cookies, or even small sandwiches) in the waiting room.
5. If you have a videotape on your company (or an HR orientation video), have it playing in the corner on a fairly large monitor. This will help sell your organization.
6. After the candidate returns their application and attached resume back to the sign-in table, have the HR people review it and take it to the appropriate hiring manager for review.
7. The hiring manager should read over the documents, go to the waiting room, announce the name, and take the person to an interview room.
8. Provisions should be made to make offers on the spot, if possible. Actual employment will always be contingent on the candidate passing reference checks, drug tests, and/or medical tests.
9. It is a good idea to try to interview everyone and not skip anyone unless there is no opening for them. Some people will come to an open house in hopes that there will be an unpublished job opening. If you have no current opening, have them fill out an application and let them go. Tell them you will keep their application on file for six months.
10. Do a follow-up analysis a few days after the corporate open house to determine the level of success achieved.

### Outside Sales People

Outside sales people are always in contact with many people and numerous companies. They usually know when layoffs are coming and who is looking for new jobs. Ask your purchasing department and any other employees who talk to these people to keep them up to date on your company's open positions.

### Outplacement Companies

Outplacement companies assist people in finding new jobs or help them with career transitions. Some companies will pay for this service for employees that they have to lay off. It is usually part of their severance package. Most of these outplacement companies will have their clients' resumes on their web site or will e-mail them to you. It is easy to go to the Internet or local Yellow Pages to get a list of outplacement companies in your area. From time to time some of these companies will have an open house and invite employers who are hiring to come to their facility to meet their clients. Once again, this is an excellent opportunity to see a lot of candidates in a short period of time.

### Colleges, Trade Schools, and Private Colleges

Almost all private colleges have outplacement departments for their graduates. Many of these organizations will have access to both present and past graduates. This will give you access to entry-level graduates and graduates with few years of experience. Intern programs are another way to "try before you buy." If you have continuing recruiting needs in specific areas, an ongoing intern program is an excellent method to "grow your own" employees.

### Reference Sourcing

Another method of recruiting staff is to go through the files of past interviews and recent hires and gather all of the references and contact each one of them again. They can be asked for additional names or they may be interested themselves in a position.

### Direct Mail

In some situations, a direct mail (or e-mail) campaign will bring in some excellent talent. Contact your sales and marketing departments and have them contact trade show management of any recent exhibits or conferences they have attended. Some of these managers will provide a complete attendee list of the show. This database will usually have the titles and address of each attendee. Lists can also be purchased from professional marketing firms for people in your area. A letter with the job description and corporate background information can be sent to the job titles that best match your openings. If e-mail addresses are available, it will be even easier and faster to send it out.

### Outsourcing

You may get to the point where there is just too much to do inside the company so you will need to go outside to get assistance in order to meet those tight time frames. There are four different possibilities for this type of assistance.

In the first possibility, contingency search firms will get your job description and provide you with a stack of resumes for you to review. The search firm will schedule interviews with the candidates that you select. If your company ends up

| Leading Drivers of HR Outsourcing | |
| --- | --- |
| Access to Greater Expertise | 77% |
| Improvement in Service Quality | 46% |
| Potential Cost Savings | 48% |
| Shift (change) in HR Priorities | 11% |

*Source:* HR Department Benchmarks and Analysis Survey, 2005–2006. Available at http://www.bna.com/special/hrpromo/highlights.pdf. Accessed September 14, 2005.

hiring the candidate, you will pay the contingency search firm anywhere from fifteen to thirty-five percent of the new hire's first year's income.

Pros of using contingency search firms:

- There are no out of pocket costs until you hire
- There is a fast response if they have a large database of people
- It is good for small number of searches or easy-to-find positions

Cons of using contingency search firms:

- It is expensive
- The same candidates you have are also being sent to your competitors
- You have to do all of the prescreening
- Some firms get a little aggressive and push unqualified people

When you are looking for contingency search firms look for the following:

1. Verify that they have been in business for a while
2. Get references
3. Only work with firms who cater to your industry
4. Carefully review their contracts
5. Get their fees in writing
6. Verify what the firm will do if your employee leaves in the first ninety days. Will they repay the fee or provide you with another candidate?

The second possibility is contract (hourly) recruiting. Contract recruiters are usually paid on an hourly basis, usually anywhere from $50 to $90 per hour paid twice a month. They may come in-house and work directly out of your facility or they may work from their own offices. Contract recruiters usually interview the hiring manager, search for candidates, perform preliminary interviews with them, verify salary requirements, and judge corporate culture fit. The resumes are then sent to the hiring manager. Interviews are established and coordinated by the contract recruiter. They also remain the communications focal point with the candidate through the entire process.

Pros of using contract recruiters:

- Hiring manager and HR do less recruiting
- Fewer interviews to the point of hire
- Low cost of hire (for five and up openings)
- Better quality of people hired in shorter time frame

Cons of using contract recruiters:

- Immediate outlay of cash
- A lot of inexperienced contract recruiters are ineffective
- Not good for small number of openings
- Typical contract is for 90 to 120 days

When you are looking for a contract recruiting firm look for the following:

1. Verify that they have been in business for a while
2. Get references
3. Only work with firms who cater to your industry
4. Get a contract and ask for an escape clause (usually two weeks' notice)
5. Get their fees in writing
6. Ask for a project manager to be your primary contact
7. Request a status report or meeting every two weeks

The third possibility for outsourcing is the retained search firm. Retained search firms are used if you are looking for one or two unique or upper-echelon employees. The search is typically for 90 to 120 days and the fees are thirty to forty-five percent of the first year's salary. These firms usually want thirty percent to start, thirty percent when the interviews start, and the final forty percent when the hire is completed. They will interview the hiring manager and top management, search for candidates, perform preliminary interviews, verify salary requirements, and judge corporate culture fit. The resumes are then sent to the hiring manager. Interviews are established and co-ordinated by the retained search firm. They also remain the communications focal point with the candidate through the entire process.

Pros of using retained search firms:

- Good way to rifle shoot a search
- Usually find excellent candidates

Cons of using retained search firms:

- High cost
- Only good for unique or one to two position searches

The fourth possibility for outsourcing is the temporary agency. Some temporary agencies can provide professional part-time help, such as in accounting or information services. This may help take some of the pressure off HR until they find full-time help. Some temporary agencies provide "temp to perm" services, in which you can try people out for ninety days and hire them if they work out. If you do hire them full time, you will be charged a conversion fee. This fee is normally twenty to twenty-five percent of the first year's salary. The fee may be less the longer you keep them working on contract as a temporary employee.

Pros of using temporary agencies:

- You get to "try before you buy"
- Temp employees can usually start full time almost immediately
- If the first one does not work out, there is a pool to draw from

Cons of using temporary agencies:

- Hourly prices high
- Conversion to full-time employment costs can be high

When you are looking for temporary agencies look for the following:

1. Verify they have been in business for a while
2. Get references
3. Only work with firms who cater to your industry
4. Carefully review their contracts
5. Get their hourly and conversion fees in writing
6. Verify the number of weeks and number of hours per week that the temp will work

### Industry Experts

When doing searches for high-level people, look into the industrial experts. These people can be found because they write books, articles, and white papers, give seminars, and are directors of boards. They also may be involved with charities and other nonprofit organizations. Most trade publications have reporters, editors, and publishers who also know all of the industrial experts. Contact your marketing department and see if they can get a list from the trade publications. Most reporters are very good at passing on such information.

## INTERNET RECRUITING

The Internet is the best tool for recruiting, bar none. You can look for people all over the world then turn around and e-mail all of them to see if there is an interest. Fast and inexpensive, it allows you to cover a lot of area in a relatively short time frame. There are pay-for sites like http://www.Monster.com, which has over twenty million resumes online, and a specialized search engine to look for titles, keywords, specific education levels, locations (usually by zip code), even individual names. There are other not-for-pay sites like http://www.passivecandidates.com/. As the Internet matures, it is harder and harder to find free sites, but they are out there. There are also specialized sites for such professions as nursing, finance, computer science, construction, truck driving, and so on. At the end of this chapter you will find a list of both free and pay-for web sites.

There are two additional methods for looking at web sites: "x-raying" and "peeling back." These are methods of finding information in the web site such as resumes, phone lists, directories, e-mail addresses, and other information that is usually invisible to typical web visitors.

X-raying sites can find hidden information. A lot of the information that resides on web sites is not linked to the main web pages available to the casual visitor. Search engines may find these pages on a web site, which would otherwise be invisible to you. If you want to x-ray a web site to see of they have a software engineer, go into Google and type in *site:websitename "software engineer."* Do not use www or http in the address, just the site name. This will return all the pages in the web site that contain the term "software engineer."

Peeling back is a process that should be used is a site contains information that is of interest to you. When you peel back a web address, you delete the last part of the web address up to the first forward slash (/). This will show you all of the information that is contained in that folder. For example, if you find that the name John Smith is in a location like this: www.sitename.com/directory/S/Smith-john/ if you peel back the address to www.sitename.com/directory/ you will end up in the main directory where you will have access to the entire directory.

Another Internet use is job postings. The Internet has numerous (both free and pay-for) sites where you can post your job openings. Since you will be competing with other companies looking for talent, be sure that you create a good posting that sells itself. Include corporate background information, locations, information on relocations, travel, and include a concise job description. Special note: Keep a list of all your job postings so they can be removed after the position had been filled.

Passive candidates are people who do not post their resumes on the Internet or outwardly look for jobs. They can be found, however, by using the Internet to search special trade chat rooms, white papers, articles, seminars, or trade associations.

Using the Internet to recruit is time consuming and can be difficult at times. The more you use it the more you learn and the more candidates you find. It is a good method to find people but should be used with the other tools outlined in this chapter.

### Using Google for Internet Recruiting

A lot of Internet recruiting will cost anywhere from $100 to $1,000 per month. However, with a little practice, you can search the Internet for free using Boolean logic.

#### Keyword Searching

The magic to keyword searching is finding out all the different words that could point to what you are seeking. For example, after you have used the keyword *Resume* you can also do additional searches using these words:

- "Curriculum Vitae"
- "CV"
- "Vitae"
- "BIO"
- "Qualifications"
- "Objective"
- "Experience"
- "Education"
- "References"
- "Work History"

It is interesting how many resumes on the internet do not have the word *Resume* on them. Most candidates assume that the format and layout is self-explanatory.

The following words could be used in a job openings site instead of resumes:

- "Submit"
- "Opening"
- "Recruiter"
- "Send"
- "Benefits"
- "Requirements"
- "EOE"
- "Apply"
- "Services"

These words should be used with the Boolean NOT function. This will help bring you more resume hits and fewer job opening hits.

When searching the Internet for resumes, use this list to add to your Boolean logic string. Remember, the most important key words should be at the beginning of the string. Listed below are the key areas to include in your searches.

- Job Titles: There are many different ways to identify a sales person," so using job titles for the search may prove difficult unless you have a unique title in a unique industry. The sales position may have various titles such as Sales Rep, Account Rep, Sales Associate, or Sales Coordinator. Competitors' job boards may provide you with usable job titles that may be standard in your industry.
- Tools and Proficiencies: This is especially good when searching for programmers or engineers. You can use such terms as "C++" or "Java" or "Flip Chip" Engineers or "Embedded Systems" Engineers.
- Jargon: Make sure that you use both the term and its acronym because you do not know which one the applicant used. The acronym PSM means "Process Safety Management"; either term may be on the resume.
- Skills: This is another area that will work if you can condense it down to skills that are necessary in the job such as, "must be able to read blueprints" or "must have injections molding skills."

---

**Definition: Boolean Logic**

---

(bool'ē-ən loj'ik) (n.) Named after the nineteenth-century mathematician George Boole, Boolean logic is a form of algebra in which all values are reduced to either TRUE or FALSE. Boolean logic is especially important for Internet searches because it fits nicely with value searches. Another way of looking at it is that each search variable has a value of either TRUE or FALSE.

---

- Certifications: Most certifications are easy to find if you use both the acronym and the entire term, for example,
  Project Management Professional OR PMP
  Certified Associate in Project Management OR CAPM
  American Society for Quality OR ASQ
  Other certifications use only a generic designation such as:
  A+ Certification
  Cisco Certified
  Oracle Certified
- Competition: Additional keywords that should be used are competitors' names. After your interview with the hiring manager, he will supply you with the company's competition, which can be used in the keyword search. The search can look like "ericsson" OR "qualcomm" OR "sprint"
- Organizations and/or Associations: Candidates will usually list all professional organizations they belong to on their resume. These can be an excellent way of locating resumes that may have IEEE, Association of Practicing Certified Public Accountants, or the American Society for Quality. With a little research, you can find all the relevant associations in your own area.
- Locations: The Internet is worldwide so you must narrow down your search to specific locations. This can be done by city, state, zip code, or area code. If you are looking at an entire state, use both the entire name and abbreviation such as CA or California.

The following is an example of how to use Boolean logic and the Google search engine to find a candidate on the Internet. We are going to use Google simply because it is currently the most popular search engine. First, we need to define some simple rules:

### Boolean Logic in Google

| Boolean Operator | In Google |
|---|---|
| AND | automatically defaults to |
| OR | \| |
| NOT | – |

| Boolean Modifiers | In Google |
|---|---|
| "exact phrase" | "exact phrase" |
| (parenthesis) | do not need in Google |

| Field Search Command | In Google |
|---|---|
| intitle: | brings back documents with the words in the title of the document |
| inurl: | brings back documents with the words in the url |

Now we are going to run a search in Google using the rules listed above. For this example we are looking for a resume of a CFO (Chief Financial Officer) who lives in the Chicago area and we want to exclude job postings. The following would be our search term:

intitle:resume "cfo" or "chief financial officer" il | illnois 312 | 708 | -submit –reply

Special Note: Google is not case sensitive; therefore, you don't need to worry about using lower case or upper case for your keywords. However, other search engines may be case sensitive and it is a good habit to read the search information for each search engine.

- The term *intitle:resume* is being used to bring back only documents that have the word resume in the title.
- The words "cfo" and "chief financial officer" have been put in quotation marks because we wanted Google to know it was a phrase and that those two terms need to come back in exactly that order. They are separated by the OR statement because we want to look for either "cfo" or "chief financial officer" in the resume.
- Because we know that some people use the state abbreviation IL and others will spell out Illinois we connect these two with the OR symbol.

- To narrow down the location even further we will look for either of the area codes 312 or 708.
- Sometimes you will want to get rid of certain documents coming back in your search results. You can do that by putting the "-" symbol in front of a word that you want to exclude, such as "*submit and reply.*"
- Remember that you do not need to type AND in Google; it automatically defaults to AND function.

You can use other search engines such as www.alltheweb.com, www.yahoo.com, www.lycos.com, www.teomoa.com, or www.find .com. Please note that the Boolean logic functions typically are slightly different from search engine to search engine. Each search engine will define its particular Boolean logic functions in its definitions section.

---

### Case Study 6-1: Two Successful High-Tech Searches

*The high-tech recruiting firm had two very difficult searches. The first one was for three Cisco router technicians. They had to be "Cisco Certified" and reside near Austin, Texas. The second search was for a Software Certification Manager, another tough position to recruit. The recruiters were well trained in using the Internet for searching these challenging positions. After just two days of internet searching, they found a small association of certified Cisco technicians located right outside of Austin! Out of ten members in the association, three were recruited in short order. The other headhunter found an organization in Colorado that was created just for software certification and configuration management personnel. After posting a free ad, the recruiter got a resume from a very qualified applicant who lived only 10 miles from the client company. All the "tough" job openings were filled in a very short time frame.*

---

### Using AltaVista for Internet Searching

#### Flipping
Flip searching allows you find Internet web pages that are linked to a certain web site. The concept is that the employees of a targeted company will have their resume linked to their employer's web site. Here is a step-by-step process to do flipping:

1. Go to www.altavista.com
2. Go to "Advanced Search"

3. Select the button next to "Search with...this Boolean expression"
4. Type in the box link:www.xyzcorp.com where www.xyzcorp.com is the web site you want to flip
5. Click on the Search button. Now when you do this you will get a lot of results, many of which are not resumes or what you want. So to do flip and look for resumes, type in the following
6. link:www.xyzcorp.com AND (title:resume OR url:resume)
7. This should return resumes associated with the key web site
8. Taking it a step further, you can add a job title. Type in link: www.xyzcorp.com AND (title:resume OR url:resume) AND "CFO"
9. Or you may type in link:www.xyzcorp.com AND "ceo" OR "Chief financial officer" AND title:resume
10. If you want to see resumes associates with AT&T and want to narrow your search to a specific geographic area such as New York City, use the area codes like this link:www.att.com AND title:resume AND url:resume AND (212 OR 646 OR 917)

*X-Raying*

The concept of x-raying a web site is to find all pages that are attached to it. Basically it searches Internet pages inside a web site, especially useful for searching universities and other organizations that might have resumes posted on site. It is also good for doing research on potential candidates and target source or client companies.

1. Go to www.altavista.com
2. Go to "Advanced Search"
3. Select the button next to "Search with...this Boolean expression"
4. Type in the box host:www.xyzcorp.com, where www.xyzcorp.com is the web site you want to flip
5. Click on the Search button. The results will give you a list of pages within that web site.

*Peeling*

The idea of peeling is used when it looks like you have gotten deep into a web site location and you need to "peel back" until you get to another location. For example, if you used flipping or x-raying to get you to the page www.xyzcorp.com/internalonly/directory/staff/joesmith/ you might want to peel back to www.xyzcorp.com/internal

only/directory/staff/ or www.xyzcorp.com/internalonly/directory/ to see if you have found the organization's list of employees.

It is a good idea to get into the habit of always looking at the web site addresses that you have been sent in order to determine where you are. In addition, sometimes you will recognize that it is a location that you have already investigated and can quickly move on.

### Anchor Search

The anchor search concept is that there are corporate web pages that include some revealing words as part of the address, such as "view resumes."

1. Go to www.altavista.com
2. Go to "Advanced Search"
3. Select the button next to "Search with...this Boolean expression"
4. Type in the box anchor: "view resumes" and "software engineer" or a company 's name
5. This will take you to any site using the words as part of the address

### Advanced Techniques

Now if you want to find resumes of anyone associated with AT&T in the New Jersey area use this format incorporating the local area codes: link:att.com AND title:resume OR title:resume OR url:resume OR url:resumes AND 908 OR 732 OR 973 OR 201 OR 609 AND nj AND new jersey

Please note that if any of these numbers show up within the resume, that resume will also be brought up.

### Boolean Logic Rules for the AltaVista Search Engine

You can use these terms for both basic and advanced web searches using the www.altavista.com search engine. For advanced searches, type these into the free-form Boolean box (located in the advanced search section).

AND Finds documents containing all of the specified words or phrases. Peanut AND butter finds documents with both the word peanut and the word butter.

OR Finds documents containing at least one of the specified words or phrases. Peanut OR butter finds documents containing either peanut or butter. The found documents could contain both items, but not necessarily.

---

### Firewalls

You may not find information using flipping, x-raying, peeling, or some of the other search engine functions. Many companies have started putting their employee lists, attached employee resumes, organizational charts, phone lists, and the list behind firewalls in order to prevent recruiters from accessing these data.

---

### Blogs

The Internet has a new activity now called "blogging." A blog is simply a journal (personal, corporate, political, topical, educational, legal, etc.) that is available on the web. The person who keeps a blog is a "blogger." The term "blogging" is defined as the activity of updating a blog. Blogs are typically updated daily using software that allows people with little or no technical background to update and maintain the blog on a web site. Postings on a blog are almost always arranged in chronological order with the most recent additions featured at the top of the page. Blogs give people a platform to establish their level of expertise in their areas. This can be a lot more revealing than a typical resume. It also gives bloggers more space to describe themselves, which is difficult to do on a resume. Job search blogs were developed to give job seekers another way display their talents and skills. They were first launched in 2004. This is another excellent area to look for people or find out more about them.

---

NOT Excludes documents containing the specified word or phrase. Peanut NOT butter finds documents with peanut but not containing butter. NOT must be used with another operator like AND. AltaVista does not accept "peanut NOT butter" in quotation marks; instead, specify peanut NOT butter without the quotation marks.

domain:domainname Finds pages within the specified domain. Use domain:uk to find pages from the United Kingdom, or use domain:com to find pages from commercial sites.

host:hostname Finds pages on a specific computer. The search host:www.shopping.com would find pages on the shopping.com computer, and host:dilbert.unitedmedia.com would find pages on the computer called dilbert at unitedmedia.com.

link:URLtext Finds pages with a link to a page with the specified url text. Use link:www.myway.com to find all pages linking to myway.com.

title:text Finds pages that contain the specified word or phrase in the page title (which appears in the title bar of most web pages). The search title:sunset would find pages with sunset in the title.

url:text Finds pages with a specific word or phrase in the url. Use url:garden to find all pages on all servers that have the word garden anywhere in the host name, path, or filename.

## Internet Recruiting Web Sites

Here are just a few Internet sites available for recruiting. Some are free and some charge a fee.

| | |
|---|---|
| www.AbsolutelyHealthcare.com | www.HotJobs.com |
| www.AllRetailJobs.com | www.IEEE.com |
| www.CareerBank.com | www.IMDiversity.com |
| www.CareerBuilder.com | www.JobCircle.com |
| www.CareerExchange.com | www.Jobing.com |
| www.CareerJournal.com | www.JobScience.com |
| www.ccJobsOnline.com | www.JobsinLogistics.com |
| www.CollegeGrad.com | www.JobsinME.com |
| www.CollegeRecruiter.com | www.JobsinNH.com |
| www.ComputerJobs.com | www.JobsinRI.com |
| www.Computerwork.com | www.jobsinthemoney.com |
| www.ConstructionJobs.com | www.JobsinVT.com |
| www.ConstructionJobStore.com | www.JobDirect.com |
| www.Craigslist.com | www.JobOptions.com |
| www.DICE.com | www.Jobs.com |
| www.eFinancialCareers.com | www.JobServe.com |
| www.EmploymentGuide.com | www.JobWeb.com |
| www.ExecuNet.com | www.LawEnforcementJobs.com |
| www.Experience.com | www.LocalCareers.com |
| www.FinanceJobSites.com | www.MarketingJobs.com |
| www.FlipDog.com | www.MEDSTER.com |
| www.GetaGovJob.com | www.Medzilla.com |
| www.Hcareers.com | www.Monster.com |
| www.HealthCareerWeb.com | www.MonsterTrak.com |

www.NationJob.com
www.RegionalHelpWanted.com
www.SecsintheCity.com
www.Showbizjobs.com
www.techies.com
www.TelecommutingJobs.com
www.TopUSAJobs.com
www.TriadCareers.com

www.TrueCareers.com
www.Vault.com
www.Vets4Hire.com - (Military)
www.WITI4Hire.com - (Women)
http://finance.groups.yahoo
.com/group/recruitingjobs/
?yguid=163429068

Note that Internet sites and links come and go so any links referred to in this book may or may not be active by the time you access them.

## Form 6-1
## The Search Plan Checklist

❒ Yes    ❒ No    ❒ NA - Advertising
❒ Yes    ❒ No    ❒ NA - HR Resumes
❒ Yes    ❒ No    ❒ NA - Employee Referral Programs
❒ Yes    ❒ No    ❒ NA - New Employee Sourcing
❒ Yes    ❒ No    ❒ NA - Internal Corporate Postings
❒ Yes    ❒ No    ❒ NA - Re-Approaching Candidates Who Rejected an Offer
                              in the Past
❒ Yes    ❒ No    ❒ NA - Professional and Trade Associations
❒ Yes    ❒ No    ❒ NA - Patents and Trademarks
❒ Yes    ❒ No    ❒ NA - Past Employees
❒ Yes    ❒ No    ❒ NA - Job Fairs
❒ Yes    ❒ No    ❒ NA - Competitive Companies' Layoffs
❒ Yes    ❒ No    ❒ NA - Corporate Open House
❒ Yes    ❒ No    ❒ NA - Outside Sales People
❒ Yes    ❒ No    ❒ NA - Outplacement Companies
❒ Yes    ❒ No    ❒ NA - Colleges, Trade Schools, and Private Colleges
❒ Yes    ❒ No    ❒ NA - Reference Sourcing
❒ Yes    ❒ No    ❒ NA - Direct Mail
❒ Yes    ❒ No    ❒ NA - Outsourcing
❒ Yes    ❒ No    ❒ NA - Contingency Search Firm
❒ Yes    ❒ No    ❒ NA - Contract (Hourly) Recruiter
❒ Yes    ❒ No    ❒ NA - Retained Search Firm
❒ Yes    ❒ No    ❒ NA - Temporary Agency
❒ Yes    ❒ No    ❒ NA - Industry Experts
❒ Yes    ❒ No    ❒ NA - Internet Recruiting—Paid
❒ Yes    ❒ No    ❒ NA - Internet Recruiting—Free

**Form 6-2**
**Staffing Status Report**

| Staffing Status Report as of MM/DD/YY |
| --- |
| Note: Latest Candidate information in **BOLD** |

**Overview of Activity**



*Job Title:*                 *Hiring Mgr:*

*Status: (Use the following in the chronically order they occur)*

- Open (Date)
- Updated Job Description *(Date)*
- On Hold as of *(Date)*
- Cancelled as of *(Date)*
- Closed *(Date)*


**JOB DESCRIPTION**



**Candidates**

(continued)

**Form 6-2**
**Staffing Status Report** *Continued*

---

| *Job Title:* | *Hiring Mgr:* |
|---|---|

*Status: (Use the following)*

- Open (Date)
- Updated Job Description
- On Hold as of *(Date)*
- Cancelled as of *(Date)*
- Closed *(Date)*

**JOB DESCRIPTION**

**Candidates**

# CHAPTER 7
## *Resumes*

You are now at the point where you have resumes to start reading. If you are posting to or advertising in some high-profile web sites or publications, you may have to review hundreds of resumes in a short period of time. If you are working on a lot of different job openings, it is usually better to group the resumes by position and read them in that manner. By "batching" the resumes you can concentrate on each unique job opening, which is easier than jumping back and forth between jobs.

### THE FIVE-POINT QUICK CHECKLIST

You now want to create a Five-Point Quick Checklist of key elements for each position. This should include the following:

1. Title(s)
2. Knowledge, background, and top three attributes (as defined by the hiring manager)
3. Experience level
4. Education and/or certification
5. Special requirements such as travel or relocation

## *Title*

Some job titles vary from company to company. Your "Jr. Accountant" job title may be called an "Accountant I" in other companies, so don't get hung up on having an exact title match. After you have read a few dozen resumes you will have a good idea what the current job titles are in the outside world. If you do not recognize the title, continue to read the resume and evaluate the relative experience. Don't be like the recruiter who gave the receptionist a stack of resumes to divide by job title only to be told at the end of the day that there were no matches when there were actually dozens!

## *Knowledge and Background*

Evaluating the knowledge, skills, and abilities necessary to perform the job is, of course, the primary criterion for resume review. The first and most important match will be the three attributes as outlined by the hiring manager. If they only have one or two of the attributes, hang on to them anyway because you made have additional openings in the future or the hiring manager may change the job description.

## *Experience Level*

Make sure the experience level is as per the job description. This may take a phone call or e-mail to determine exactly how much expertise the applicant has in each area. Most people will put the last title they had in the job. However, they may have only held that title for a part of the five years they were employed. There should be a continuing increase in responsibilities seen in the resume. Some people are individual contributors who get into management, don't like it, and end up becoming individual contributors again. So major changes in their responsibility may not be a problem. This is especially true in a tough economy where you have to take what is available.

## *Education and/or Certification*

Education and certification is another area to quickly check. Some companies demand at least an undergraduate degree for consideration; other companies will take experience over degrees. It just depends on the organization. The colleges that the candidate graduates from can also make a good impression to the resume reader. An MIT engineer graduate will be moved high on the list of acceptable resumes. Some people will write down that they are working on a degree. This may or may not be true because it always looks good on a resume. These people should be questioned about what last classes were taken for this degree or certification and when they plan to graduate or become certified.

While college degrees are easily verifiable, certifications are a little bit different. Some HR managers and hiring managers wonder out loud, "Is certification is a true measurement of achievement, or just a memory exercise?"

Some certifications are valuable and should not be dismissed lightly. There are currently over 450 certifications on the market and more are coming out every year. Many of them are in the technical areas but more and more are popping up in other industries such as retail and insurance. Security certifications are now very widespread. Certifications are a good starting point, but are not a substitute for hands-on experience. Some certified people are still poor workers who think that certification is their career cure-all. Some people will become certified by memorizing answers, buying the answers, or actually buying the certification. Recruiters and HR departments can challenge and expose these cheaters by working with such companies as Caveon (www.Caveon.com) that were formed to detect and prevent test fraud. There are certain pros and cons of certification and here are some of them.

### Pros

- The certification vendor gains credibility
- HR and hiring managers feel reassured
- Certification may verify candidate knowledge level
- Certification assists in bridging to new specialty
- Certified staff are usually more productive
- Certification shows the candidate has initiative
- Certification helps level the recruiting playing field when comparing resumes and backgrounds

### Cons

- Certification is not a substitute for hands-on experience
- Certification is not a free ride
- Some certified candidates are still poor workers
- Certification is not a career cure-all or one-shot solution

- Some only got certified because they were promised higher-paying jobs

Recruiters need to be certification aware and know exactly what their hiring managers' certification requirements are. Remember, the best candidate will have a balance of experience and certification.

### Special Requirements

There are some job requirements that may end up to be "deal killers," such as relocation or travel. The position may require fifty percent travel and the resume may say nothing about travel. In most instances, you will have to contact the applicant to find out if travel is an issue. In other cases, you may have a resume that states "no travel" or "no relocation." Some people feel very strong about these areas while other people will not make up there minds until they hear about the job. Bottom line is that if there is a possibility of a problem, make the call or e-mail and find out!

Be sure to highlight any information that is key to the job. As you read through the resumes make sure that you write any questions that you have as you go through the paperwork. This will save time later because you will not have to reread the resume and rethink the process. Make sure that you do not write down anything that you would want the candidate or a lawyer to see.

If you have a particularly strong applicant, make sure to note that at the top of the resume so the applicant stands out. Also, remember that some resumes have been on the Internet for a while and the candidates may have already found jobs. If this is true, you can always ask them if they know anyone else who is looking.

By focusing on just these five key elements you will be able to scan through many resumes rapidly. This will also keep you from sending resumes of applicants who are not fully qualified to the hiring managers.

## READING RESUMES BETWEEN THE LINES

Sometimes applicants do not express some of their best talents in their current resumes. It may take a little analysis in order to see if they are real candidates. Some do not put down the exact titles of the jobs that they are seeking. They just list all their experience and hope that someone in HR will figure out where they belong. These resumes must be studied to determine if their background matches your job description. On the other hand, some resumes are blatantly phony. They will have a lot of impressive facts that are all unable to be proved. They will list companies that have gone out of business and references that can no longer be verified. So be ye aware!

Another area to look at is their past companies. Have they been with competitive companies or related vendors? Have they been with start-up or large companies? This may give you an idea of what size company or what area of the industry they feel more comfortable in. Remember that they may want be looking at your small company because they want to get away from large companies.

Look at their working time frames for each job to see if there are dates that are overlapping. Look for any lapses in time between jobs or situations where it appears the candidate went "backward" in their career growth. You have to be careful when looking into this area, however. Only a few years ago, if a person stayed at a company for only one or two years, they were branded as a "job hopper." That was before the current economic condition, including the dot-com bust. People had more loyalty to their employers in the past. In the twenty-first-century business climate, there is little loyalty. People now have resumes with short work times because companies merge, down size, go out of business, or move out of the area. Job hopping may be a good reason to contact applicants and find out what their story is all about. They may have a real problem or simply be the victim of a strange economy.

Review their educational records and any certifications that they have earned. Someone who is continuing to take classes may be that aggressive employee you have been looking for. There are so many methods to get educated nowadays that even the busiest people have opportunities to better themselves. Ongoing education is always a good trait to have in an applicant.

Sometimes the cover letter does not reflect the same information that may be on the resume. The cover letter may refer to the job description's request for five years' experience while the resume only shows two years' worth. This may be an indication that the applicant is just modifying the cover letters for each job opening or they may not have updated their resume recently.

The salary history should reflect the experience level. There are people out there that got into higher salary ranges by job hopping or just convincing their employer that they were worth more. If you

> Almost 52% of all job applicants have some form of misrepresentation on their resumes.
>
> *Source:* "Are Your Applicants Lying About Their Degrees?" *Smart Hire Newsletter.* Available at http://www.adphire.com/newsletters/degrees.htm. Accessed September 14, 2005.

bring someone into the organization above your compensation range, you will have a salary compression issue with your current employees. These hires are typically not happy with anything other than high salaries and will leave your company to make a few more dollars elsewhere as soon as they have the chance.

Some resumes will have information of a personal nature. Maybe they are members of certain organizations or have a list of their hobbies. This may or may not be useful to you—it usually just takes up room on the resume—but it can give you some idea of what the applicant does in their spare time. It can also be useful during interviews to start small talk or just to break the ice before the interview starts. Interviews are difficult for most people so talking about their hobbies can get them to relax before starting the interview process.

Poorly written resumes should not be automatically discarded. It is never good to have typos and grammar problems in a resume, especially with today's spell and grammar check programs. But there are some applicants out there who just are not good with writing a resume. While this could reflect on their communications skills, it should not eliminate them from the interview process. A lot of creative people cannot spell but are superstar employees.

Personal activity shows an interest outside of work. This could be a problem if there is too much emphasis on outside events. This may indicate that the candidate neither gives work high priority nor has extra time for those priority projects. It could also just be a sign that they have a balanced life. You will need to find out during the interview.

## RESUME TRACKING AND HANDLING

Before we get into the details of reading resumes, let's talk about the categorizing, processing, and handling of resumes. The resume handling process is significant because you don't want valuable people to get lost, and it is important that everyone is contacted and handled professionally.

Make sure that you categorize each resume when you read it for the first time. This will save time and reduce resume handling. The resume tracking categories are:

1. YES—Meets basic Five-Point Quick Checklist
2. MAYBE—Resume will take closer scrutiny or a phone call
3. NO—Does not meet Five-Point Quick Checklist (too light or too heavy)
4. OTHER—Resume is for a completely different position than the one advertised

The resumes can be electronically filed or physically filed if they have been faxed or mailed to you.

The YES group will typically be contacted by the recruiter for a phone interview or sent to the hiring manager, depending on the established process. Some hiring managers want to see all the resumes before the applicant is contacted. Any resumes sent to the hiring manager should be tracked by name, date sent, and position placed. It is important to get feedback from the hiring manager on the viability of the resume as soon as possible. Other companies are also trying to hire this person so time is of the essence.

The resumes in the MAYBE group will have to be read in depth to determine if they meet the job description criteria. Since some candidates will not be able to list all experiences on two pages or have poorly written resumes, it may take a phone call to determine if the candidate is a fit for the position. Good recruiters may recognize these people and perform in-depth interviews to dig into their backgrounds and find information that was not on the resume. If, after talking to the applicants, you feel there is a fit, have them rewrite and resubmit their resumes for submission to the hiring manager. The MAYBE file should eventually be empty, moving the resumes into one of the other categories.

The NO file will have people who are not qualified for the position. It also will include applicants who are too light or too heavy for the current opening. It is smart to keep these people on file because the job description may change after a few applicants have been interviewed. The hiring manager may decide that the position needs more experience (or less) than first thought. If this happens, you will have a small pool of applicants to start interviewing and do not have to start from scratch. In addition, some of your job openings will need a support staff to assist them so some of lightweights may become very valuable.

The *OTHER* file is all of the resumes that do not come close to what you are looking for. For example, you advertised for a CFO and you got a resume from a warehouse supervisor. Some applicants will see that you are hiring and hope that you are hiring in their professions also. From time to time you may actually have an opening for these types of people and it could work out for everybody, but normally you only have the positions that have official authorized requisitions. All resumes that are not going to be considered should be responded to with a "no thank you" or "rejection" letter, postcard, or e-mail then filed in the HR department (see chapter 8). Be sure to keep an electronic or manual track of all these activities so you can follow up and make sure people are responding and the paperwork is moving through the system. By tracking this activity you can drive the process and get decisions made. You do not want good resumes to disappear into the corporate paperwork maze and not be responded to.

## "CALIBRATION RESUMES"

When you are first starting a job search it is a good idea to send the hiring manager a couple of "calibration resumes" in order to make sure that you are on target with the job description. These are the resumes you feel reflect the needs of the hiring manager and will confirm that you are looking for the right person. If there is a problem with the job description, it will be obvious when you get the response from the calibration resumes. Some hiring mangers will slowly change their minds about a position and not realize it until they start reading the first few calibration resumes. Do this as soon as you get the first couple of qualified resumes and this will allow you to get quick feedback before you get to deeply into the search. Nothing is worse than searching for people that you do not really need. You don't want to waste a lot of time and money; you have to hire some superstars!

## SOLVING THE "RESUME AVALANCHE" PROBLEM

In some situations you may be overwhelmed with the response from your job postings or advertising and get hundreds of resumes. This is called the "resume avalanche" and if handled properly it can be a happy problem. It is always great to have a large pool of resumes to start evaluating. It is a difficult problem because you have so many to read. You need to get this avalanche down to a workable size so you can respond to everyone as soon as possible.

One good way to do this is to create a questionnaire consisting of all the preliminary questions that you will be asking in

> 12% to 23.3% of candidates who send resumes to this firm misrepresent their education.
>
> *Sources:* Barbara Mende "Employers Crack Down on Candidates Who Lie," CareerJournal.com. Available at http://www.careerjournal.com/job-hunting/resumes/20020606-mende.html. Accessed September 14, 2005.

your first interview. E-mail this questionnaire to all potential applicants with your five or six most important questions at the top. The applicants who are really interested will fill it out and quickly return it to you. The applicants who were just testing the market probably won't bother to do so. This action will do two things. First, it will reduce the number of active applicants to a workable size and second, it will give you a fast analysis of each applicant. By doing this, it will help you to either start scheduling interviews or forward some calibration resumes to the hiring manager. If you do not hire someone from the group that responded, you can always resend the job description to the people who did not respond to your questionnaire and see if there is still some interest.

## COMMUNICATIONS

As always, communications are very important during the resume review process. Applicants should know that their resumes are being reviewed. Hiring managers must know what kind of activity is going on with the recruiter. The recruiter must make sure that the hiring manager gets back to him as soon as possible on the calibration resumes and, later, on all the other resumes that are acceptable. Applicants who fall into the *NO* or *OTHER* category should be sent some form of communication to let them know that they did not fit the profile needed. This is the professional thing to do. No one wants to get a "no thanks" letter, but it is better than never hearing anything (see chapter 8). Without a response, applicants never even know if their resumes were received or reviewed. A response from you will at least give closure to the process and puts your company in a professional light. The applicants at least feel that they were important enough to get a professional response, even though it was a rejection.

---

### Case Example 7-1: The Never-Changing Resume

*While some people are always changing their resumes, there are a few people who never change theirs. One recruiting firm has been getting the same resume from the same applicant for over seven years! It has never changed! The resume, which is in "letter" format, quotes from monthly publications that were produced in 1985 and 1998. He goes into great detail of the types of jobs that he does not want. He also takes a couple of paragraphs explaining why he is worth $50,000/yr. In his industry, this salary would not be considered "low." The resume is never mailed or e-mailed, it is always hand delivered at the end of every year. No one in the company ever sees this person, but the resume is always found lying at the front door every year!*

---

## SUMMARY

It has been often said that "a resume is like a balance sheet with no liabilities." The only reason for having a resume is to get an interview. Some resumes are going to be long some short, some will be beautifully written while others will be tough to read. Don't be too hasty to toss resumes in the trash. There may be valuable information that you do not readily see. The applicant may have more certifications than college degrees and in some situations that will work. They may have a better background than they put on the resume. The bottom line is that the resume will more often than not be your first contact with a candidate. Use the resume and primary contact information as your guide for finding those superstar employees. You may have to do this by reading between the lines.

**Form 7-1**
**Quick Resume Checklist**

1. Job Title(s):
2. Knowledge:
3. Experience Level:
4. Education and/or Certification:
5. Special Requirements:


**Form 7-1A**
**Sample Quick Resume Checklist**

1. **Job Title(s):**
   *Office Manager*
   *or*
   *Office Administrator*
   *or*
   *Administrative Services Manager*
   *or*
   *Operations Manager*
2. **Knowledge:** *Must have background in construction industry*
   Top Three Attributes:
   *a. Must have heavy accounting background*
   *b. Must work well under pressure*
   *c. Must have supervisory experience*
3. **Experience Level:** *8–10 years plus*
4. **Education and/or Certification:** *AA degree or equivalent years in experience, Notary Public would be ideal, but not required*
5. **Special Requirements:** *No travel or relocation*

# CHAPTER 8
## *The Interview*

Interviews are difficult for everyone involved. You may have hiring managers who have little time or do not know how to interview or you may have candidates who have not interviewed in a long time. The recruiter should be the focal point and must make sure that the candidate is treated as "special" and professionally. Even if the candidate is not hired, they should have had a positive experience. This will help give the company a positive and professional reputation. If the interview appears to be going badly, the recruiter should explore the situation and see if it can be saved. Sometimes just another interview will solve the problem.

---

### Case Example 8-1: Saving a Bad Interview

*The company wanted three people supporting three different areas but did not have enough work for full-time. The recruiter found a great candidate who could handle all three areas and was a great people person. But there was a problem, because the candidate was scared of interviewing. The recruiter tried to coach the candidate before the fateful day, but the interview was a disaster. The recruiter remembered that this candidate always did better if he had a second interview. After numerous telephone calls, the company reluctantly agreed to bring him in again. The second interview went great because the candidate felt more relaxed. He was hired and ended up being one of their best and most productive employees.*

---

## INTERVIEW PREPARATION

### Preliminary Information

When applicants are contacted for the first time, it is essential to determine if their salary is within the range established in the job requisition. You must also verify that there is not a problem with travel and/or relocation, if applicable. A final question is on availability. Are they ready to make a move or are they on a project that they will stay with for another three months? Some sales people may not want to leave until the end of the quarter or fiscal year. If any of these areas are a problem, you need to learn about it as soon as possible and not waste your time chasing someone who you cannot afford.

### Who Performs the Interviews?

The first step in the interview process is to determine who will be on the interview team. The recruiter or someone in the HR department should be the first (and last) person that the candidate always sees. The hiring manager will take the lead in creating the hiring team. If the opening is for an individual contributor, the hiring manager and their staff will probably do the interviewing. If the candidate will be frequently interfacing with other department(s), their managers should be added to the interview team. Openings for management personnel should have other middle and upper managers in the hiring team mix. For openings in upper echelon positions such as a CFO, the hiring team may include the Board of Directors, third-party auditors, or, if applicable, the venture capital group(s). Make sure that there are backup interviewers in case someone gets sick or busy. Some small to medium-sized companies will have the applicants do a courtesy interview with their president or CEO. Just a fifteen-minute meeting is an excellent way for your company to impress the candidate and also allow your president to see the quality of the candidates being interviewed.

### Group Versus Individual Interviews

Some companies like to have a group or panel interview the candidate. This can help expedite the process and usually makes it easier for everyone to discuss the results right after the interview. The group interview concept may get better information out of the candidate because someone interviewing may ask for clarity to an answered question. On the other hand, this may put additional pressure on the candidate because the questioning can become intense. It is also important that the more outspoken members of the group do not "hijack" the interview and not let others ask their questions.

Other employers like to do one-on-one interviews because there is a different dynamic from that of the group. The one-on-one interview is perceived as much more informal than the group interview. It is felt that more information on the candidate's personality can be perceived in the one-on-one interview.

### Phone Interviews

Some hiring managers want to do the first interview over the phone. It allows them to get a first impression without having to get all the other staff involved in the interview. If the phone interview goes well, the hiring manager can bring the applicant in for an in-depth person-to-person interview. In addition, the hiring manager may not need as much face-to-face interview time. It is better to schedule phone interviews after hours. In this age of small office cubicles, it is impossible for a candidate to have a private conversation anymore. The hiring manager should find acceptable time frames for the candidate and should initiate the call.

### Interview Scheduling

Each person interviewing should be asked how much time they will need for their interview and the best time to interview. Some need thirty minutes, most need one hour, some will go over an hour. It is important to keep the interview on schedule as much as possible. Remember that everyone is busy and if you get too far off the schedule, some may not be able to interview. This means you may have to bring the applicant back or forgo the interview with that person. Be sure to factor in time between interviews. You don't want the times to overlap too much or the last person will not have any time at all. Be sure to tell the applicant how long the interview process will take. If you have many people involved in the interviewing process, you may want to break it into two separate days or have a group interview. Don't forget to think of the candidate. Interviewing is tough, and the longer the interviews, the tougher it is for the applicant. In addition, if the interview goes over lunch time, make provisions for feeding the applicant.

This can be done by HR or one of the other interviewees. Some interviewers like to interview over lunch because they say that it is easier on the applicant. By the way, the company should always pay for lunch.

HR or the recruiter should be in charge of moving the applicant through the interview process during the day. You don't want applicants sitting in the lobby all by themselves, waiting for something to happen. Remember, their time is valuable, too! An Interview Schedule Form (see Form 8-1) will let everyone know where the applicant should be at any time during their visit.

### Evaluation Form

Each person who interviews should fill out an Evaluation Form (see Form 8-2). This will help determine the final evaluation of the applicant. The hiring manager and recruiter can evaluate the answers from the same baseline of these questions. The evaluation form has a rating number system for easy analysis and a checkbox at the bottom for the final decision of the interviewer.

### The Interview Package

Every interviewer should get an interview package from HR or the recruiter the day before the interview. The package should consist of the following:

1. Interview Schedule Form (see Form 8-1)
2. Job Description (see chapter 5)
3. Applicant's resume
4. Evaluation Form (see Form 8-2)
5. Application and related forms

The job description is an important document to have as part of the package because some of the interviewers may not know what the applicant is interviewing for.

HR should contact the interviewers via phone or e-mail the day before the interview to remind them of their appointment.

### Interview Questions

Before the actual interview, make sure that you outline the questions that you are going to ask. These should include any questions that you wrote during the resume review. The following are sample questions:

### Sample Interview Questions

1. What motivates you?
2. How well do you take direction?
3. How do you handle criticism?
4. Do you enjoy doing routine tasks?
5. What is your management style?
6. How do you work in a team?
7. How do you approach a typical project?
8. How do you operate under stress?
9. How creative are you?
10. How do you get the best from people?
11. How do you resolve conflict in your team?
12. What would your boss or coworkers say about you?
13. What do you dislike most at work?
14. Why have you been with your present employer so long / short a time?
15. If applicable, why have you had so many jobs in such a short time?
16. What are your most significant achievements?
17. If you could start again, what career decisions would you make differently?
18. Do you consider that your career so far has been a success?
19. How long would it take you to make a useful contribution to this company?
20. What do you think are the key trends in this industry?
21. Describe a situation that, in hindsight, you could have handled better.
22. What sort of decisions do you find difficult to make?
23. Describe a situation in which your work was criticized.
24. What sort of people do you find it difficult to work with?
25. How much do you think you're worth?
26. Does this job sound interesting to you?
27. What appeals to you most about this job?
28. What appeals to you least about this job?
29. How would you feel about assisting other departments on short-term projects?
30. How do you think you will fit in here?

---

### Questions You Cannot Ask

It is illegal for an interviewer to make hiring decisions based on anything personal or not directly job-related. Off-limits questions include (but are not limited to) the following:

1. Age
2. Citizenship/national origin
3. Race/color
4. Gender/marital status
5. Children/childcare
6. Physical, health, or mental disability
7. Religion/creed
8. Residence ownership
9. Military service
10. Organizations/societies/activities (outside of professional associations)
11. Height/weight
12. How long the candidate will work before retirement or pregnancy

So keep away from questions like this and stick to your acceptable questions for each applicant. Be sure to ask the same questions of each applicant so each can be fairly evaluated.

---

## THE INTERVIEW

We are now at the point of the actual interview. You have now determined who will be giving the interviews and have the times scheduled. A list of questions has also been developed and it is time to perform the interviews. The interviewers are to determine if the applicant has the skills, experience, and knowledge to do the job. These questions can be easily answered, but even more important are these three questions:

*1. Is the applicant compatible with your corporate culture?*
Corporate culture is defined as the personality of the organization. Sometimes it is difficult to define it when you are close to it. Here are some of the elements of corporate culture to consider:
- Hours worked per day and per week
- Flextime and telecommuting rules
- Work environment
- Dress code

- How employees interact
- Degree of competition in the organization
- Is the environment fun, hostile, stressful, or a combination?
- Office space available
- Rules regarding display of personal items
- Formal training available
- Onsite perks, such as free coffee, gyms, play rooms, day care facilities
- Is the interaction between employees, managers, and top management formal or informal?

*2. Is there good "chemistry" with the applicant?*

Some hiring managers and other interviewers may report that the applicant interviewed well, but something "didn't feel right." This may be because the chemistry wasn't good between the applicant and the key interviewers. This is an important consideration but difficult to explain. Sometimes you just don't "click" with someone; it is like you are on different wavelengths. It may take a second or third interview to determine if there is a chemistry fit. If, after additional interviews, there still appears be a problem, move on to the next qualified candidate.

*3. Does the applicant have additional talents that can be used in the future?*

Remember to review the resume for additional talents other than those you need for this opening. Ask the applicant about these additional talents and if they are agreeable to spreading their knowledge throughout the organization.

### Nonverbal Communication

During the entire interview process the candidate will be giving you nonverbal "messages" that can be very revealing . These will be in the guise of nonverbal communications. Here are just a few to watch for and evaluate:

1. *The handshake.* This will be your first encounter with the candidate. If you receive a limp, unenthusiastic hand in return, it is not a very good beginning. The handshake should be firm and natural. Don't worry if it is slightly damp. Interviews are nerve-racking and people do get nervous.

2. *Posture.* The candidate should stand and sit erect. They should exhibit some energy and enthusiasm. A slouching posture looks tired and apathetic.

3. *Eye contact.* The candidate should be looking you in the eye—not staring, but looking. Make sure there is frequent eye contact. They should not be constantly looking around the room while you are talking. Be aware if there is any nonverbal activity that conveys nervousness or a lack of confidence with what is being discussed at the time.

4. *Hands.* Gesturing by candidates is very natural, but it should be in moderation. Getting carried away with hand gestures can be distracting. Also, candidates should not cover their mouths while talking. It will appear that they are hiding something or are ashamed.

5. *Fidgeting.* Candidates should not be playing with their hair, clicking pen tops, tapping feet, or unconsciously touching parts of the body. The fidgeting may just be due to the stress of the interview or it may indicate a problem with communication.

6. *Eyes.* The old adage that says, "the eyes are the windows to the soul," has some credibility. Some people are very responsive with their eyes. When you are talking about something that they believe in or relate to closely, their eyes appear to "light up," indicating that they really understand. Other people may not show any eye response to anything that is said during the interview.

7. *Facial communication.* The face can broadcast a large number of emotions. Some people, however, are very good at presenting a "poker face," especially during negotiations. It is important to watch the face very closely, especially after asking a key question.

Nonverbal communication should be only part of the overall interview process, but use it as an important basis for evaluation.

### Don't Let the Candidate Take Over the Interview

Some applicants have their own agenda and try to take over the interview by asking and answering their own questions. Other applicants are experts at not answering your questions and redirecting you to other areas. Make sure you get each question answered before you move on. If you are not sure of the answer, ask again. Keep asking until you get an answer. As the interviewer, it is your responsibility keep control of the dialogue and interview process.

## The Care and Feeding of the Applicant

If applicants have been treated professionally, they will tell ten associates. If they feel they were treated poorly, they will tell twenty! That is the reality of interviewing PR. You must look at the interview process as also being a PR process for your company. Anytime you interface with the outside world, you (as your company) will leave an impression. This can be a good or bad impression, depending how you treated the applicant. Even if you do not end up hiring the applicant, you want them to feel they were treated professionally. No one wants to sit in a lobby waiting and waiting. No one wants to wait for a long period of time after the interview to find out the results. Make sure you ask applicants if they want something to drink, especially between each interview. Remember, they are going to be doing most of the talking. In addition, give them easy access to the restrooms between interviews. Nothing is worse than trying to interview when you feel uncomfortable. Make certain that applicants have copies of all relevant corporate brochures and make sure HR has supplied them with company and benefits information. Applicants should be impressed by the professional manner in which they were treated.

Before the candidate leaves, get their impression of the interviews. Ask them if they have any questions, ask if they think the position is a good fit, find out if they think they can work with all the people they interviewed with. Give them your business card and tell them to call you at any time if they have any questions. Then tell them your next step in the process. Are you interviewing more people? When will you make your decision? Set up a time frame in which you will contact them and then make sure to get back to them even if you don't have any updated news. You want to keep them captivated until you know if they are your first, second, or third choice. It is best not to send out rejection letters until you are sure your primary applicant has accepted your offer.

One final note about the application form: Nobody wants to fill out that long, boring application, but it is a legal document that you must have in your file. Make sure that they fill out the form completely and sign it. If your organization performs any type of drug testing or reference checking, there will be additional forms to be filled out and signed. The best thing to do is to get the application (and other forms) to the candidate before the formal interview. The best way to do this is to have the forms downloadable from your web site. The alternative is to mail the application and other forms directly to the applicant. You must have these documents finalized before you can make a formal offer, so make sure you have them before the candidate leaves the first interview.

---

### Case Example 8-2: The Badly Treated Candidate

*The candidate was not overly thrilled to be scheduled for a 4:45 interview on a Friday, but he was glad to get it. He got to the company at 4:40 and told the receptionist who he was supposed to see and she called the secretary to announce his arrival. It was now 5:00 and most of the company was filing out and leaving for the weekend. By 5:20 the receptionist cleaned up her area and told the candidate that she was sure they would be out to see him any minute. By 5:40 the candidate was not sure what to do; it appeared that most of the organization was gone and there was no active phone in the lobby. At 5:50 the director stuck his head into the lobby and asked the applicant if he was there for the interview. "Yes, I am", he replied. "I am sorry. My secretary is mad at me and didn't tell me you were here!" After that, the candidate had no interest in working for a company that treated him like that.*

---

### Sell the Job During the Interview

It is a good idea to contact all of the interviewers before the interviews begin and tell them to help sell the job and the organization to the applicants. While you are trying to evaluate the applicant, they are trying to decide if they want to work for you! So as soon as you start talking to them, you should have a few key selling points about your company. Sometimes it is good to reach into the positive points of the corporate culture to sell the company. People want to hear about opportunities in the organization and it is never too early to sell them. If the applicant does their homework, they will be looking at your web site and will see all your products or services, press releases, and annual report, if you are a publicly held company. So if there is anything that is negative on the web site, now is the time to explain it away. Most corporate problems are temporary and there are plans in progress to solve the problem. The job opening may be part of that plan.

## Evaluating the Results

After the interview, you want to meet with the interviewers as soon as possible to get their impressions. Gather the evaluation forms and talk to each one individually to determine how he or she felt about the candidate. There may be questions from the interviewers such as, If they are so good, why aren't they making more money? Or Are they worth that much money? In some situations, an applicant may have worked for the same company for a long period of time. If it was during a bad economic time, salary increases would only be two to four percent per year, resulting in an applicant having a lower than expected salary. It is not a good idea to try to get these people "on sale." At some point in time they will find out that they can make a higher salary than they originally thought and move on. Conversely, if it appears they are making too much, HR should do a quick salary evaluation to see if their salary levels are reasonable. With superstar applicants, you usually get what you pay for.

If someone had a bad "gut feeling" about the applicant, he or she should talk to the other interviewers to see if any of them had the same feeling. If there is any doubt, it is imperative that you bring the applicant back for a second or even third interview to see if there is any change. Some of us have a problem trying to evaluate someone in just one hour, and additional interviews are a necessity. You do not want to have a good applicant slip through your fingers. On the other hand, you don't want to hire someone who will not work out.

The job description may change after the first few interviews, especially if the hiring manager feels that something important was missing from the first interviews. If major changes are made to the job description, it may be necessary to completely restart the search. This may happen more often than one would think and may be embarrassing for the hiring manager. But, in reality, this is the only way some hiring managers can understand what they really need. It is more important to get the right people into the right positions than it is to hire quickly. So let the hiring managers determine exactly want they want and work toward filling their positions. If the job description needs updating, the recruiter or HR should make the changes and redistribute it to all the job posting firms, outplacement firms, and all other locations.

In summary, the recruiter or HR department should be the driving force behind the interview process; they should ensure that all the documentation is acquired and disseminated properly; and they should gather all the opinions of the interviewers and determine what next steps should be taken.

---

### Case Example 8-3: Strange Reasons for Eliminating Candidates

*Some hiring managers have strange reasons for eliminating candidates. One hiring manager refused to see the applicant because she was fifteen minutes late. Her valid excuse of an accident on the freeway fell on the deaf ears of the hiring manager. In another situation, the hiring manager was not interested in the applicant because he had his initials on the sleeves of his white dress shirt. "Anyone with a big 'ego' like that will never work for me!" yelled the hiring manager. And, finally, an HR manager dismissed the administrative assistant candidate because "She blinked too much! I think she was trying to hide something," she said. Further investigation revealed that the candidate had just gotten contacts and her eyes were still getting used to them.*

---

## The Rejection Letter

As soon as you know that the applicant is not going to be chosen for the position, they must be contacted. In most situations, the recruiter will call the applicant and tell them that they did not make it. It is also important to send an official "no thank you" or rejection letter. We have composed a sample letter for you to use or you can adapt it to your own situation (see Form 8-3).

**Form 8-1**
**Interview Schedule Form**

---

**Name of Applicant:** _____  **Position:** _____

HR Contact/Recruiter _____  Phone Ext. _____

| Time | Interviewer | Phone Ext. |
|------|-------------|------------|
|      |             |            |
|      |             |            |
|      |             |            |
|      |             |            |

Note: If you cannot interview at the time noted or have a conflict during the day of the interview, contact the HR Contact/Recruiter at the top of the page as soon as possible!

**Form 8-2**
**Interview Evaluation Form**

Name of Applicant: _____          Position: _____

Interviewer: _____

Rating Scale: 1- Unsatisfactory.....Does NOT meet position's requirements
                 2- Satisfactory.......Fully meets position's requirements
                 3- Outstanding......Exceeds position's requirements

**EXPERIENCE**                                                          **RATING**
How does the candidate's previous experience relate
to the current position's essential duties and responsibilities?        _____

**JOB KNOWLEDGE**
How well does the candidate's skills, working knowledge,
and abilities meet the job description?                                  _____

**COMMUNICATIONS**
Does the candidate express themselves well and present
ideas clearly, concisely, and with confidence?                          _____

**PERSONALITY**
Evaluate the candidate's sincerity, conscientiousness,
responsibility, and integrity                                           _____

**MOTIVATION**
Does the candidate demonstrate iniative, leadership,
drive, project focus, and commitment?                                   _____

**CAPABILITY**
Does the candidate appear resourceful, logical,
imaginative, poised, and capable?                                       _____

**OVERALL POTENTIAL**
How well does the candidate's background and experience
meet the requirements for this position?                                _____

**FUTURE TALENT POTENTIAL**
Does this candidate have potential for advancement or
multiple talents?                                                       _____

**FINAL EVALUATION**
❐ Recommend for current opening
❐ Do not recommend for current opening
❐ Recommend for future positions

**COMMENTS**
_____
_____

Signature _____                    Date _____

**Form 8-3**
**The Rejection Letter**

*ACME Industries*
*123 Main St*
*Anywhere, USA*
*12345*

John Smith
North South St
Main place, USA 54321

Dear John:

Thank you for the interest that you have shown for the position of (Job Title) and for taking time out of your busy schedule to interview at ACME Industries.

At this time, we have selected a candidate whose abilities and experience more closely match the particular needs of this position.

However, we will keep your resume on file, and will contact you if another position becomes available. We encourage you to keep us in mind whenever you are seeking a job.

Once again, thank you for your interest in ACME Industries

Kindest regards,

Representative, Department

# CHAPTER 9

## The Job Offer

The most critical point in the recruiting cycle is making the offer. Management typically feels that when an offer is made it will be automatically taken. This, of course, is not true, but there are actions that can be taken to minimize the number of rejected offers. The recruiter should start discussing an offer package with the candidate as soon as the hiring manager voices an interest. For legal reasons, it is important not to make an actual offer early in the process, but to pose it in a manner such as, "If you were offered $86,000 per year with a twenty percent bonus based on performance, and could start in two weeks, what would be your response?" By having these discussions early in the process, the recruiter will hope to determine the following:

1. What the candidate's "hot buttons" are, for example title, salary, stock options, bonus programs, future potential, and so on.
2. That there are no related problems such as relocation, travel, insurance, and the like that can cause a problem.
3. That the candidate may just want to take a written offer back to their boss to force a raise or promotion.

At this point, the recruiter can usually sense if the candidate is actually serious about the position and has real potential. In addition, early talks like this frequently reduce the negotiation time frame.

## COMMUNICATIONS BEFORE THE OFFER

After the interviews are completed, you want to keep in communication with the candidate(s) and let them know how things are progressing. You also want to find out if they are going on any other interviews or getting any other offers to consider. You may have to make adjustments to your offer if it looks like you are in competition with other employers.

## THE OFFER LETTER

The offer letter is also known as an employment contract and it is a formal, legal contract. It must be signed and dated by the candidate to be legitimate. You must make sure it is accurate and approved by all key management before it is sent out or presented. Here are the key elements to the offer letter:

### 1. Opening

The opening should be upbeat and positive. Show the candidate that you are excited about the possibility of their joining the team. Talk about looking forward to their contributions and presence in your company. Show them that you are eager for them to start as soon as they can. This is also a good time to continue to sell the company with some positive points and exciting news.

### 2. Title and Reporting Structure

Include the candidate's formal title and who they will be reporting to. If this is a management position, add the department(s) and/or staff that will be reporting to this person. If there is a dotted line of responsibilities to another person, include that in this section. Also, indicate if this is a part-time, full-time, exempt, or nonexempt position.

### 3. Location and Hours of Employment

If the company has a campus with a number of buildings, include a map with the location where the new employee will work or check in on the first day. During the interview process, candidates may never see the actual work location because a lot of interviewers will use a

---

### Exempt Versus Nonexempt Job Status

Your status as an exempt or nonexempt employee does not depend on how the employer characterizes you, but rather on your job duties. Simply put, exempt employees are exempt from overtime pay or both minimum wage and overtime pay provisions. You are actually paid a salary. Exempt employee duties fall into one of three categories: executive, administrative, or professional.

Nonexempt employees are paid on an hourly basis and may be available for overtime. These are usually nonmanagement, nonsupervisory positions that have less responsibility than exempt positions. Every state is different, so check the minimum wage, overtime, and other wage and hour laws for your individual state.

---

conference room to hold the interviews. Many companies now have flextime or start at 7:30 or 8:30; this may help employees with the daily commute. Be sure to let the new employee know when you expect to see them and what the normal business hours are for your company or individual department. If the employee is going to telecommute, add the times that they will be "off campus" to this section.

## 4. Compensation

This section will outline all compensation to be presented to the candidate. This includes annual salary, bonuses, commissions, overrides, and the like. If you are hiring a sales person, attach a copy of the commission plan that they will work under. These plans are normally good for twelve months or until the end of the company's fiscal year.

## 5. Perks and Benefits

This section will outline any perks or benefits such as car allowances, cell phone, notebook computer, and so on. If the new hire will to telecommute and work out of their home office, detail other items provided such a separate business line, Internet hookup, phone, fax machine, furniture, and so on. Also, list all the other perks the company may have available such as:

- Vacation, sick time, personal leave time formula
- Expense reimbursement
- Stock options

- Professional licenses
- Professional memberships
- Profit sharing
- Incentive programs
- Employee referral programs
- Retirement plans
- Cafeteria-style insurance programs
- Employee Stock Ownership Programs (ESOP)
- Educational reimbursement
- Child care availability or assistance
- Assistance with elder care
- Wellness programs
- Weight loss programs
- Stop smoking programs
- Free health screening
- In-house gym or gym membership discounts
- In-house massage therapy
- Sponsor employee sports teams
- Sponsor employees' children's sports/arts/musical programs
- In-house post office
- Discounts on products or services provided by company
- Store membership programs
- Dry cleaning service
- Discounts for in-house cafeteria
- Access to take-home meals

### 6. Termination Clause

"At-will" employment is an employment relationship in which either party can terminate the employment relationship at any time, for any reason that is permitted by law, with no liability. If the employer decides to let the employee go, that's the end of the job—and the employee has very limited legal recourse to fight this type of termination. This clause should be reviewed by legal counsel or your corporate attorney before it is used in offer letters. It should also be very prominent in the *Employee Handbook*.

### 7. Reference Checking and Drug Testing

If your company has a mandatory drug testing program as a criterion for employment, make certain it is stated in the offer letter and declare

---

### At-Will Employment

Unless the employer gives some clear indication that it will only fire employees for good cause, the law presumes that you are employed at will. It is still imperative that if you have decided to be an at-will employer, you will include the statement in your offer letters and in the *Employee Handbook*. It should read some thing like this:

"All personnel are employed on an at-will basis. This means that employees have the right to terminate their employment at any time, for any reason, with no notice and the company can also terminate the employment at any time with or without cause and with or without notice. All policy statements, procedures, manuals, or documents as well as statements by an employee or representative shall not in any way modify the at-will policy."

---

that all offer letters are null and void if the drug test is not passed. Your company may require in-depth reference checks that look into the candidate's finances and criminal history, verify college degree and certificationa, and confirm previous employment.

### Reference Checks

It is always a good idea to do some form of reference testing on all candidates to whom you are going to make an offer. The areas to check are the past three companies where they were employed, three past supervisors, two peers, their degree(s) and/or certification(s) and indirect reference information (see below). See Form 9-2, Reference Check Form for a list of questions.

- Company reference checks—Companies do not give out very much information due to the fact that so many were sued when they gave less than positive reports. Most companies nowadays will only verify the dates of employment, job title(s), and if the person was fired for "cause," but they usually will not go into detail about why the firing occurred. This will at least give you some input.
- Supervisors and peers—Past supervisors are a good source of information. If they are no longer working for the company, they may provide a more detailed account than if they were still under the corporate directives. Peers can give you a good idea of how the candidate worked as a team player and how they got along with others. Bosses and supervisors don't always see all of the different moods that people show to their peers.

- Degrees and certifications—Because some surveys have reported that nearly as many as twenty-three percent of applicants lie about their degrees or certifications, it is a good idea to verify them. They can be easily checked by contacting the colleges and or businesses that are listed on the resume.
- Indirect reference information—If you have a list of companies that your own key employees have worked for, you can compare it to the candidate's companies and see if anyone knew the candidate when they worked there. You can also keep a list of companies that your other business contacts have worked for and see if they knew of or heard any information about your candidate. If you have good contacts in your industry via associations, organizations, HR mangers, or personal contacts, you may be able to find out some indirect information about the candidate.

---

### Case Example 9-1: Indirect Reference Information

*The search for a customer service manager was almost over. The interviews went well but the references could never be fully checked out because some of the people could not be contacted. The HR manager decided to authorize an offer letter and sent it to the president for final approval. When the president got the offer package, he called the HR manager and asked to see the candidate's resume. After reviewing the resume, the president informed the HR manager that he had known this person from another company, and he had not achieved half of the accomplishments that he claimed he had. When questioned about references, the HR manager admitted that he had not contacted anyone because they were all out of town or never returned his phone calls. The candidate ended up with a rejection letter instead of an offer and a lot of problems were averted.*

---

### Drug Testing

If your company has a mandatory drug testing program as a criterion for employment, make certain it is stated in the offer letter and declare that all offers are null and void if the drug test is not passed. Also, if you have a drug testing policy, make sure that *all* new employees in your company get tested regardless of position. Be sure to make every effort to keep the results of drug tests confidential. Only persons with a need to know the results should have access to them. Be advised, however, that test results may be used in arbitration, administrative hearings, and court cases arising as a result of the employee's drug testing. Also, results will be sent to federal agencies as required by federal law. If the employee is to be referred to a treatment facility for evaluation, the employee's test results will also be made available to the employee's counselor. Some companies that have ongoing drug problems will do random testing on all employees. All drug testing policies must be included in employee manuals and posted.

---

**Checking of References**

47% Check references during the interview process

30% Check past employers and/or schools listed on resume/application

*Source:* "Resume Padding Is Commonplace, According to New York Times Job Market Research, *Business Wire,* May 29, 2002. Available at http://www.findarticles.com/p/articles/mi_m0EIN/is_2002_May_29/ai_86424405. Accessed September 14, 2005.

---

### Employment Verification Services

Due to the fact that there are some states that make it easy for the applicant to file lawsuits based on reference check problems, many companies are using third-party services. Most of these companies know what to do to keep from getting sued and what information they can legally obtain.

In some states (such as California), employers are required to give copies of all third-party investigations to the subject employee or applicant if requested. Employers must also have signed documentation from the candidate giving permission for third-party background checks (Cal. Civil Code §1786). In California, this authority was given by the legislature's Investigative Consumer Reporting Agencies Act (ICRA). It requires employers to give notice of any investigation conducted by a third party. For example, if the employer hires a consultant or attorney to prepare a background verification report on the two finalists in a job placement process, each of those individuals would have to be given written notice in advance of the investigation. If any candidate provides a written request for the final report, the employer must provide it.

Failure to comply with the California requirement will cost $10,000. That is, of course, in addition to the $25,000 penalty that can be assessed on a consumer reporting agency the employer hires to conduct the investigation. Punitive damages are also possible if a court decides the violation was willful or grossly negligent. Multiply the number of job applicants you see each year by these numbers and you have the potential financial impact of this new law on your organization.

Here are some ideas to keep your company from getting penalized:

- Work only with third-party background checking firms that are aware of these requirements; if they aren't, you might consider using someone else.
- Prepare a written authorization form you can have employees and applicants sign when you must conduct a background check. Get help from your management/labor attorney to be sure it meets all legal requirements of your state.
- Be sure you maintain accurate records of all background checks and that you archive files for at least two years. Each file should have a notation about the date requested and the date that you provided the individual with a copy of the background check report.

Reference checking is just one input to your final hiring decision. If you get a negative reference check or a previous boss who is slow to respond to key questions, you might want to dig a little deeper and see if there may be some truth to your suspicions. Remember that some people are such professionals at lying they are rarely discovered. They have told the lies for so long they even believe them. If you feel uncomfortable with a response, ask for additional references. You could even bring the candidate back for additional interviews in which they are confronted with any discrepancies.

## 8. Moving Allowance

If the applicant is allowed a moving allowance, it must be totally outlined in the offer letter. Some companies pay for the move totally, some will also pay for limited motel stays, and some will even assist in the selling of the old home and repurchasing the new home. Make sure that the exact cost (or not to exceed costs) and time frames are outlined in the job offer letter.

## 9. Limit Response Time

Never make the response time to the offer letter "open ended." It is essential to limit the amount of time for which the job offer is valid. You want to be able to apply pressure to the candidate to make a decision. You do not want the candidate to be able to use your job offer to "shop around" at other companies. Characteristically, four to seven days is plenty of time to get a decision from the candidate. If there are legitimate continuing negotiations, this time frame may be lengthened.

---

### Nondisclosure Agreement

A standard nondisclosure agreement should read something like this:
*"Employee agrees not to use, disclose, or communicate, in any manner, proprietary information about Employer, its operations, clientele, or any other proprietary information, that relate to the business of Employer. This includes, but is not limited to, the names of Employer's customers, its marketing strategies, operations, patents, programming source codes, manufacturing processes, or any other information of any kind which would be deemed confidential or proprietary information of Employer. Employee acknowledges that the above information is material and confidential and that it affects the profitability of Employer. Employee understands and that any breach of this provision or of any other Confidentiality and Nondisclosure Agreement, is a material breach of this Agreement and could result in possible legal action against the employee."*

---

## 10. Nondisclosure

Make sure that you contact legal counsel or your corporate attorney to create a standard nondisclosure paragraph for the new employee to sign (see nondisclosure sidebar for additional details).

## 11. Trademarks, Copyrights, and Patents

All employees give up their rights to trademarks, copyrights, and patents when they are being paid by an employer to develop said items. Nevertheless, it is important for them to know and agree to this clause. Have your legal counsel or corporate attorney approve these clauses (see sidebar for additional information).

## 12. Probationary Period, Performance Reviews, and Salary Reviews

As a rule, the typical probationary period is the first ninety days of employment, at which time a decision is made if the employee will be kept on or let go. Performance reviews are customarily conducted every six or twelve months, while salary reviews normally take place yearly.

## FINAL INTERNAL SIGNATURES SIGN-OFF

After the offer has been created and you have verified the content, your corporate policy may dictate that it goes through a formal upper

### Trademarks, Copyrights, and Patents

Here is a standard paragraph that may be used in an offer letter:

*"Employee understands that any copyrights, inventions, or patents created or obtained, in part or whole, by Employee during the course of this Agreement are to be considered 'works for hire' and the property of Employer. Employee assigns to Employer all rights and interest in any copyright, invention, patents or other property related to the business of the Employer. Special note: If Employee is working on patentable material it is recommended that the company enter into a separate patent assignment agreement."*

management sign-off process before being sent out. This is a good cross-check procedure to use routinely. However, if the offer is within the job description and requisition parameters, the hiring manager and HR representative may be the only signatures required.

## THE VERBAL PHONE OFFER

Once the offer has been approved, a verbal offer can be made. This can be done by the hiring manager, recruiter, or HR representative, depending on corporate policy on who makes job offers or on whoever has the best relationship and been in closest communication with the candidate.

Whoever makes the verbal offer should have a copy of it in front of them so they can read off all the key parameters of the offer. Try to get an answer to the offer while you are on the phone, but expect the candidate to say they want to see it in writing and think about it before they make a decision. They can either pick up the offer package at the company or you can mail it overnight to them. You want to get the written offer package into their hands as soon as possible.

---

### Case Example 9-2: Impressing the Candidate

*The hiring manager really wanted to get the IS Manager he had been interviewing on board as soon as possible. The candidate was a real superstar who had exactly what the company needed. He knew that the candidate had at least two other offers and was waiting for a third. He wanted to do something unique to impress the candidate and get him to join the company. The hiring manager remembered that the candidate had a "courtesy interview" with the president of the company. He asked the president if he would make the phone call offer. The president agreed and the candidate was so impressed that he was called directly by the president of the company, he accepted the offer over the phone and started two weeks later. To this day he has been a superstar employee.*

---

## THE OFFER PACKAGE

The hardcopy offer package should consist of the following:

1. Two copies of the signed offer letter (one for the company and one for the candidate)
2. Corporate benefits and insurance information
3. Employee handbook
4. Company literature
5. Corporate backgrounder
6. Self-addressed stamped envelope

You want to make sure that candidates have all the information that they need to make their decision and feel good about it. The package should be sent for next-day delivery by USPS, FedEx, UPS, or other local carrier to ensure delivery. Use their tracking service or contact the candidate to ensure that the package has been delivered.

## NEGOTIATION

Every company handles the negotiation process a little differently. A decision must be made as to who will be the sole company focal point for the negotiations. This person must have the authority to make company hiring decisions.

Typically, if the recruiter has done their job properly, there should be little negotiation after the initial offer is made. In order to expedite the hiring process, it is recommended that the first offer you present to the candidate is your best offer. If you do this, you should have little to negotiate. However, candidates may feel there may have been a misunderstanding, or just feel that the first offer is never the best offer, so they may want to negotiate. Here are some perks that you can offer as additional negotiation points:

1. Salary review in three to six months—If candidates feel that the salary is too low, you can offer to give them a salary review in three to six months (based on performance) instead of the customary twelve months. This allows candidates to prove themselves before the increase takes effect. Be sure that the exact dollar amount is in the offer letter so there is no confusion later.
2. The sign-on bonus—Another method that works well is to offer a one-time sign-on bonus. The size of the bonus depends

on the salary level of the candidate. The sign-on bonus is especially good for sales people because it gives them an opportunity to make up for future commissions that they will lose when moving to a new company.

3. Added vacation time—Increasing the candidate's vacation from the standard two weeks to three weeks for the first year of employment is another way to "sweeten the pot." The candidate may have accrued many weeks of vacation from her last company so this may be a good and inexpensive way to get her to accept the offer.
4. Contract to perm—If the candidate is not sure it is a good fit, and you think it is, you might offer to put them on contract for three to six months. After that time, you can both decide weather you want to make it permanent or go your separate ways.

Candidate who continually want to negotiate, may be trying to delay in giving you an answer because they are either renegotiating with their current company or talking with other companies. At some point, you may need to give a final offer tied to a short response time. If the candidate does not accept and still wants to negotiate, walk away; they do not appear to be serious about the offer and may have a hidden agenda.

## REJECTION

The candidate may also reject the offer. If this occurs, try to find out the exact reason(s) that the offer was rejected. There are four common reasons that candidates decline formal offers:

1. The current company gives the candidate a counteroffer with a promotion, more money, or a new position
2. Candidate decides not to make a change because they feel secure in their established environment
3. Candidate feels that the challenge, money, growth, or responsibilities are not acceptable
4. There exist other lifestyle problems such as a difficult commute, relocation, insurance coverage, or travel

## BACKUP CANDIDATES

It is essential that you always have a backup candidate. You never know if the primary candidate will accept the job or not, so keep that secondary candidate interested—you may need this candidate and you don't want to have to start the search all over again. The backup candidate does not have to know that they were the second choice. They will be happy to get an offer. If you do not have a backup candidate, keep working the search process until you get a few more people in the pipeline. Never assume that the candidate you have made the offer to will take it.

## ACCEPTANCE

Once the candidate verbally accepts the offer, it is very important to obtain the signed offer letter. Some companies like to have the candidate come back to the corporate offices to sign the offer. If this is not convenient, have them send the signed agreement back to you using a self-addressed stamped envelope. Always inform the hiring manager and all the other people involved in the interview process when the candidate accepts the position. Also, let them know the new employee's start date.

The recruiter should contact the candidate every few days before the official start date to ensure they have not changed their mind or are being swayed by other late offers. You want to make the candidate feel that they made the right decision. The longer the start time, the more important it is to contact the candidate every few days, just to let them know there is still an interest.

---

### Case Example 9-3: The Candidate Who Got Away

*The candidate accepted the job offer for the senior sales position and was supposed to start in two weeks. The search was very difficult because the industry was booming and good quality people were hard to find. The interview process was fast, but complex, and negotiations took longer than normal. After the signed offer letter was received, no one from the hiring company contacted the candidate; they just assumed that she would show up for work in two weeks. Unbeknownst to the new company, the candidate was contacted by a competitive company on the Friday before the Monday start date. She actually was interviewed over the weekend. She accepted the new offer and started that Monday at the competitor. It took the first company four days to catch up with her and find out what happened.*

---

## DELAYS AND LAST-MINUTE PROBLEMS

You can always expect to have some type of delays and some type of last-minute problems. Some may be major and some may be minor. Everything, however, needs to be investigated, such as failed drug tests, questionable references, misinformation on the resume or application form, or unconfirmed degrees. The verification of this type of information is normally done in parallel with the actual offer letter, so these problems may not appear until the offer is accepted. Always give the candidate the benefit of the doubt, confront them with the problem, and try to find out if a mistake was made. There may be very simple and legitimate answers to these problems. On the other hand, you may discover that the problems are authentic and the offer must be rescinded. Additional delays may occur because of missing of signatures or key management staff being out of town. If this is the case, make certain that you contact the candidate and inform them of the delays.

## SUMMARY

The job offer procedure is probably the most crucial part of the entire recruiting process. The recruiter must be on top of it at all times and continue to drive the process every step of the way. Communication must be consistent and accurate at all times. The candidate must feel that they are really wanted and not feel that they are being ignored. You must always treat them in a courteous and professional manner. If you have followed all of the other recruiting steps in this book, the job offer and acceptance will go smoothly and you will have your superstar!

**Form 9-1**
**The Job Offer Package Checklist**

❒ Yes ❒ No ❒ NA - Positive PR Opening

❒ Yes ❒ No ❒ NA - Title and Reporting Structure

❒ Yes ❒ No ❒ NA - Location and Hours of Employment

❒ Yes ❒ No ❒ NA - Total Compensation Package

❒ Yes ❒ No ❒ NA - Perks and Benefits

❒ Yes ❒ No ❒ NA - Termination Clause—"At Will"

❒ Yes ❒ No ❒ NA - Referencing Checking and Drug Testing

❒ Yes ❒ No ❒ NA - Moving Allowance

❒ Yes ❒ No ❒ NA - Limit Response Time

❒ Yes ❒ No ❒ NA - Nondisclosure Agreement

❒ Yes ❒ No ❒ NA - Trademarks, Copyrights, and Patents

❒ Yes ❒ No ❒ NA - Probationary Period, Performance Reviews, and Salary Reviews

❒ Yes ❒ No ❒ NA - Corporate Backgrounder or Annual Report

❒ Yes ❒ No ❒ NA - Corporate Insurance Package

❒ Yes ❒ No ❒ NA - Employee Handbook

❒ Yes ❒ No ❒ NA - _____

❒ Yes ❒ No ❒ NA - _____

❒ Yes ❒ No ❒ NA - _____

❒ Yes ❒ No ❒ NA - _____

❒ Yes ❒ No ❒ NA - _____

❒ Yes ❒ No ❒ NA - _____

**Form 9-2**
**Reference Check Form**

Name of Applicant: _____

Reference Check by: _____ Date: _____

Name of Verifying Official: _____ Title: _____

Company: _____ Phone Number: _____

- What was his/her title or position?
- Dates of employment from _____ to _____
- Nature and length of their relationship to you
- Can you elaborate on their responsibilities?
- How did this person get along with superiors, associates, subordinates?
- Describe their initiative and strengths
- What support or training would this person need in order to be successful?
- What is your overall assessment of their skills and ability?
- What was the quality or quantity of their work?
- Assess their leadership or managerial skills
- What were their technical skills?
- Assess their oral/written communication skills
- Assess their decision-making ability
- Assess their professional conduct
- How were their employee and interpersonal relations?
- Did they have acceptable budgeting/financial skills (if applicable)?
- Why did the person leave?
- Would you re-hire them?
- Do you think the candidate can handle the following: (add job description here)
- Do you have any additional comments pertaining to their performance?

## Form 9-3
## Job Offer Letter Sample

Date
Mr./Ms. (Winning Candidate)
(Street Address)
(City, Zip)

Dear (Winning Candidate),

We are very pleased to offer you employment as _____ (Job Title), here at, located in _____, effective _____ (Start Date), reporting to _____ (Hiring Manager). This is a full-time exempt position. Our flexible working hours allow you start work any time from 7:00 AM to 9:30 AM. Standard Corporation hours are 8:30 to 5:30 M-F.

It is our feeling that your leadership strengths, teamwork, speed and winning mindset will be challenged to help us to continue to improve our environment to better serve our customers. We feel that this relationship will greatly benefit both parties and look forward to mutual future successes.

Please take the time to read through the following important information on our offer:

Your base salary will be _____ ($) per annum. You will be remunerated on a bi-weekly basis, payable through direct deposit to the bank account of your choice.

ACME Industries bonus program is a 50/50 split between individual contribution and corporate success. At your management level the total bonus program will be _____ (%) of you salary.

Along with your salary and bonus program you will be able to participate in our quarterly stock purchase program. Discounted stock prices, based upon the stock price at the beginning and end of each quarter, will be available to you. Based on your position in the company, you will be allowed to purchase _____ (shares) of stock every quarter for the next three years.

ACME Industries also offers a comprehensive benefits program that is an important part of your total compensation. The benefits program mainly includes health, life, pension and disability plans, and provides an Employee Savings Plan as well as a host of other benefits. There are currently three plans available to our employees, which are included in this package. You will have 30 days to decide which plans fit your life style.

In addition to the competitive benefits program and working conditions, the company provides development opportunities such as an Education Assistance Plan, world-class training programs and career assignments within the ACME Industries group of companies.

You will earn 15 days of paid vacation per year effective January 1, (Following Year). For (Current Year), you will earn 1.5 vacation day for every complete month worked up to a maximum of 15 days.

Our Paid Holidays are as follows:
- New Years Day
- Martin Luther King's Birthday
- Presidents Day
- Good Friday (1/2 day)

*(continued)*

## Form 9-3
## Job Offer Letter Sample *Continued*

- Memorial Day
- Independence Day
- Labor Day
- Thanksgiving (2 days)
- Christmas (2 days)
- New Years Eve

Keep in mind that as a condition of this offer, you will be asked to respect ACME Industries Employment Terms of being an "AT-WILL" company, in which either party can terminate the relationship at any time for any reason.

Non-Disclosure and copyrights, inventions or patents: The employee agrees not to use, disclose or communicate, in any manner, proprietary information about Employer, its operations, clientele, or any other proprietary information, that relate to the business of Employer. This includes, but is not limited to, the names of Employer's customers, its marketing strategies, operations, patents, programming source codes, manufacturing processes, or any other information of any kind which would be deemed confidential or proprietary information of Employer. Employee acknowledges that the above information is material and confidential and that it affects the profitability of Employer. Employee understands and that any breach of this provision or of any other Confidentiality and Non-Disclosure Agreement, is a material breach of this Agreement and could result in possible legal action against the employee. The employee understands that any copyrights, inventions or patents created or obtained, in part or whole, by Employee during the course of this Agreement are to be considered "works for hire" and the property of Employer. Employee assigns to Employer all rights and interest in any copyright, invention, patents or other property related to the business of the Employer. Special note: If Employee is working on patentable material it is recommended that the company enter into a separate patent assignment agreement.

This job offer is valid until no later than the end of business day (Date—allow for 3–5 business days) and is based upon acceptable reference checking and passing the standard drug test.

Please acknowledge your acceptance by signing the attached letter of offer and returning it to the hiring manager. If we have not heard from you by this date, the present offer will be deemed to be null and void. If you choose to accept this offer of employment, you will be expected to report to at 9:00 AM on Monday _____ (Start Date).

We look forward to your positive response to our offer and to help us make ACME Industries the premier choice of customers.

(Hiring Manager)
(Title)
ACME Industries Canada

Telephone: (Area code) (Telephone No.)
Facsimile: (Area code) (Fax No.)
E-mail: (E-mail address)

cc. (Optional)

**Form 9-4**
**Job Acceptance Letter Sample**

---

(Date)
To (Hiring Manager Name - Title, ACME Industries)
(Street Address)
(City, State, Zip)

I, (Winning Candidate's name)

have read the terms and conditions related to my employment stated in the letter of offer and I accept the position. I assure you that the information given to the Company is accurate and truthful and I am aware that a voluntary omission or a false declaration discovered after my hiring constitutes grounds for dismissal.

_____          _____

Employee's Signature                          Date

# CHAPTER 10
## New Hires and Recruiting Metrics

One of the key talent balancing concepts is the proper care and feeding of the candidate as a new employee. After working so hard to make the hire, it would be terrible to see the candidate leave due to problems that could be easily solved. The HR department should be the focal point in making sure everything is ready for the new employee and that they feel important and wanted.

---

### Case Example 10-1: Taking Care of the New Hire

*It was very difficult to find a high-caliber program manager, so after one was finally discovered and brought on board, the recruiter called the newly hired employee about a week after he arrived to see how he was doing in the new position. The new employee said, "Well, I am thinking of leaving! I have a bad cold and asked for the air conditioning vent to be shut three days ago and it is still open, so I'm leaving!" The recruiter immediately called the hiring manager and reported the problem. He said, "Yes, I do remember him asking and I completely forgot about it. I will take care of it right now!" He did and when the recruiter called back next day, the new employee was happy and content, and, in addition, becoming very productive, according to the hiring manager.*

---

---

### 80% of Employees Leave for Reasons Other Than Money

The five most frequently mentioned issues that employees say plague companies are:

1. Poor management—uncaring and unprofessional managers; managers overwork staff; managers give no respect, do not listen, put people in the wrong jobs; emphasis on speed over quality; poor manager selection processes
2. Lack of career growth and advancement opportunities—no perceivable career paths; not posting job openings or filling from within; favoritism or unfair promotions, mixed messages
3. Poor communications—problems communicating from the top down and between departments, after mergers, between facilities
4. Pay—paid under market or less than contributions warrant; pay inequities; slow raises; favoritism for bonuses/raises; ineffective appraisals
5. Excessive workload—doing more with less; sacrificing quality and customer service for numbers
6. Lack of tools and resources—insufficient, malfunctioning, outdated equipment/supplies; overwork without relief
7. Lack of teamwork—poor coworker cooperation/commitment; lack of interdepartmental coordination

*Source:* Leigh Branham, *The 7 Hidden Reasons Employees Leave: How To Recognize the Subtle Signs and Act Before It's Too Late,* AMACOM Publishers, 2005.

---

## PREPARING FOR THE NEW EMPLOYEE

The recruiter and HR should always keep in contact with the new employee for the first few weeks to make sure that they are being properly assimilated into the company and corporate culture. But there is also a lot of work to be done before the new employee arrives. You want to make sure that the new employee can be productive as soon as possible and feel respected during the corporate assimilation. The new employee will go through orientation more often than not on their first day. But it is important to carry it much further than just that day. The key goal is to have all their office equipment ready to go. The following are some of the things to consider.

### Business Cards

Have the new employee's business cards printed up before they arrive. It is very convenient for the new employee to give out their new card as they are being introduced throughout the company. Your current employees will have the new employee's card so they will know the proper spelling of the name, title, and phone extension. If the printer cannot supply the cards in a timely manner, just use your computer to print off twenty to thirty temporary cards until the official cards can be delivered.

> ### Keeping Employees Informed
>
> 41% of Employees that were not kept informed were looking for new jobs
>
> 15% of informed employees were looking for new jobs
>
> *Source:* Ann Egan, "Employees Value Effective Communication from Their Employer," Mercer Human Resources Consulting, April 2003. Available at http://www.mercerhr.com/pressrelease/details.jhtml;jsessionid=MUNKICDTVRIXICTGOU FCIIQKMZ0QUI2C?idContent=1089800. Accessed September 2005.

## Temporary Badge

Most companies will need to take the new employee's picture in order to process their company ID. If this is going to take more than a few days, issue them a temporary badge so they can get around the facility. If the facility has keyed or combination locks, make sure the new employee has access to the areas they need to get into.

## Work Area Stocked with Stationery Supplies

Select and prepare the work area, complete with furniture chosen for their management level. Be sure everything is functional and not broken. Nobody likes hand-me-downs. Stock the basic stationery supplies so the employee does not have to wait weeks to get a stapler or a pen. Make sure that the area is clean and functional.

## Computer

The most important office equipment is the computer. Make sure that the new employee has a working computer with all relevant application software installed. Verify that there is a working e-mail account with temporary passwords and connections to the Internet and corporate intranet.

## Notebook Computer, PDA, Pager

In addition to the in-house desktop computer, some employees may also be given a notebook computer. Verify that all the components are included such as charger, phone/ethernet cables, carrying case, portable mouse, and so on. Again, it should be loaded with all relevant application programs and be capable of hooking up to your company's intranet and the Internet. If you issue PDAs, pagers, blackberry, or any other tools, be sure that they are activated, include all accessories, and have product user manuals available.

## PHONES

Today's workers usually have both landline (wired) phones and cell phones, so the new employee should have activated phones with preassigned numbers. In addition, they should have all the manuals for these and any other support product that they will need. Voicemail should be set up with temporary passwords that the employee can later change. Verify that the corporate phone list in included.

## ADDITIONAL SUPPORT MATERIALS

Additional support materials may include the following:

1. Map of facility (coffee, bathrooms, area printers, location of other workers, etc.)
2. Corporate organizational charts
3. List of weekly meetings the employee will be attending
4. Schedules of status report deadlines, monthly meetings, and so on
5. Product manuals
6. Corporate and product collateral
7. Employee handbook
8. Parking pass/validation/parking lot map/assigned parking information
9. Copy of employee referral program

## WELCOMING THE NEW EMPLOYEE
### The Buddy Approach

When a new employee comes on board, select another employee (who has been there for a while), to be their buddy for the first week or two. The buddy will introduce the new employee to the people in the organization, take them on breaks and to lunch, show them around the facility, and be the starting point for any questions the new employee may have. The buddy does not have to be from the same department, just someone who can take a little time to help the new employee get up to speed and become productive.

### Sourcing the New Employee

After the new employee has been on board for a few weeks, approach them with your list of job openings and find out if anyone at his old company is interested in any of the openings. This is an excellent way to recruit. Good workers know other good workers, and if their previous company is falling apart, there may be many people looking for jobs.

### Monitoring the New Employee

It is vital to monitor the new employee closely for the first thirty to sixty days. After that, the average employee should feel at home. By monitoring the new employee you can head off any potential problems that may come up. Remember, you, HR, and the hiring manger only had a few hours with the new employee when you were interviewing them. Over the next thirty to sixty days you will be able to see how they are going to fit (or not) into the organization.

## COST-TO-HIRE CALCULATIONS AND RECRUITING STATISTICS

Management likes to know costs and statistics. One of the classic methods for measuring the efficiency of hiring is determining the cost-to-hire.

This can be easily done if you are using outside contract recruiters. Good recruiters will automatically provide you with this information. In order to assemble recruiting statistics you need to know the following:

Total expenditures, including:

- Advertising
- Job fairs

**Staffing Measurements Most Frequently Used by HR Departments**

45% Regularly Use Staffing Measurements

30% Sporadically Use Or Only On Demand

25% Do Not Use Or Do Not Know

Source: HR Dept. Benchmarks and Analysis Survey, a BNA/SHRM collaboration, 2004. Available at http://www.bna.com/special/hrpromo/highlights.pdf. Accessed

• Open house
• Internet
• Outside recruiters

Total salary for all hired employees during search.

The cost-to-hire formula is simply the total of the recruiting costs divided by the total salaries of hired employees multiplied by 100. This will give you a cost-to-hire as a percentage. For a comparison, remember that contingency search firms charge anywhere from twenty-five percent to thirty-five percent of the first year's compensation. So a $100,000 employee will cost you $25,000 to $35,000.

Based on these data, you may also calculate the following:

• Average hours per position
• Average hours per week to hire
• Cost-to-hire in dollars
• Number of hours per hire
• Number of weeks per hire
• Average salary per person during search plan

There are a number of variables that could artificially increase your cost-to-hire. One of these is the additional cost if the search had to be restarted because of a change in the job description or reorganization.

**Table 10-1**
**Sample Recruiting Statistics Report**

| | |
|---|---|
| Total Invoices | 6 |
| Total Weeks | 12 |
| Average $ per Invoice | 4,675 |
| Average $ per Month | 9,350 |
| | |
| Total Hours Worked | 374.0 |
| Average Hours per Invoice | 62.3 |
| Average Hours per Week | 312.0 |
| Total Hired | 4 |
| Cost to Hire (%) | 8.6 |
| Number of Hours per Hire | 93.5 |
| Weeks per Hire | 3.0 |

If it is possible to track the hours put in for the false start, they could be removed from the calculations and the cost-to-hire would be more accurate.

> The average hiring cost (over 31 industries) for 2004 was $4586.
>
> *Source:* "Data Bank: Annual Labor Markets," *Workforce Management Magazine,* December 2004, p. 105.

Another problem may be if you recruited part-time or contract employees. Technically, they are not full-time employees and should not be part of the calculation. But it takes almost as much recruiting effort to bring them on board as full-time people, so they should be added to the formula. Since contract fees are usually higher than salaried employees, those fees should not be used. Instead, use the mid-range salary that would be paid to a full-time employee. Another variable would be any requisitions that are withdrawn during the recruiting time frame. The cost-to-hire calculations are not an exact science, but will give management an idea of how much it is costing the company to find people.

**Form 10-1**
**New Hire Checklist**

---

❒ Yes ❒ No ❒ NA - Business Cards
❒ Yes ❒ No ❒ NA - Temporary Badge
❒ Yes ❒ No ❒ NA - Work Area Ready
❒ Yes ❒ No ❒ NA - Work Area Stocked
❒ Yes ❒ No ❒ NA - Computer and Passwords
❒ Yes ❒ No ❒ NA - Notebook Computer, PDA, Pager
❒ Yes ❒ No ❒ NA - Phones—Landline and Cell Phones
❒ Yes ❒ No ❒ NA - Map of facility (coffee, bathrooms, area printers, location of other workers, etc.)
❒ Yes ❒ No ❒ NA - Corporate organizational charts
❒ Yes ❒ No ❒ NA - List of weekly meetings they will be attending
❒ Yes ❒ No ❒ NA - Schedules of status report deadlines, monthly meetings, and so on
❒ Yes ❒ No ❒ NA - Product manuals
❒ Yes ❒ No ❒ NA - Corporate and product collateral
❒ Yes ❒ No ❒ NA - Employee handbook
❒ Yes ❒ No ❒ NA - Parking pass/validation/parking lot map/assigned parking information
❒ Yes ❒ No ❒ NA - Copy of employee referral program

---

# Glossary of Terms

**Anchor search:** The anchor search is a method of finding hidden words that are written inside a corporate Web page. This may include some revealing words as part of the address. An example would be "view resumes." See chapter 6.

**"At-Will" clause:** An employment relationship agreement adopted by companies in which either party (employee or employer) can terminate the employment relationship at any time, for any reason that is permitted by law, with no liability. See chapter 9.

**Blogs/blogging:** A journal (personal, corporate, political, topical, educational, legal, etc.) that is available on the Web. Derived from "Web log." The person who keeps a blog is a "blogger." The term "blogging" is defined as the activity of updating a blog. Blogs are typically updated daily using software that allows people with little or no technical background to update and maintain the blog on a web site. See chapter 6.

**Boolean logic:** Boolean logic is a form of algebra in which all values are reduced to either TRUE or FALSE. Boolean logic is used for Internet searches because it fits nicely with value searches. Another way of looking at it is that each search variable has a value of either TRUE or FALSE. See chapter 6.

**Calibration resumes:** The first few acceptable resumes that the recruiter sends to the hiring manager are called calibration resumes. These resumes are designed to find out if the search is on the right track and help "calibrate" the job description and search parameters. See chapter 4.

**Chain reaction turnover:** Chain reaction turnover occurs after layoffs, when employees become nervous and scared and leave the company. They go out and look for new jobs, expedite their retirement, go into business for themselves, or get out of the industry. Be aware that ninety days after your planned ten percent layoff, you could be looking at the reality that twelve to fifteen percent of the staff has actually left due to chain reaction turnover. See chapter 1.

**Contingency search:** Contingency search firms will charge anywhere from ten percent to forty percent of the first year's compensation. Payment is only made after the applicant is hired. See chapter 1.

**Contract recruiting:** Hiring an outside company that provides recruiting services based on an hourly payment basis. See chapter 6.

**Corporate culture:** Corporate culture is the personality of a company. Some corporate cultures can be expressed in their mission statements or company goals. Corporate culture is the company's ethics, core values, and beliefs. It is how management treats the employees and how the employees treat each other. Fitting into the corporate culture is one if the most important aspects of hiring. See chapter 1.

**Cost-to-hire:** Calculations to determine the exact cost to hire an individual or group of individuals. Typical expenditures include those for advertising, job fairs, open house, Internet costs, and outside recruiter costs. See chapter 10.

**Creeping job description:** Creeping job description usually occurs when the hiring manager slowly realizes that there are different or new job requirements needed for the position than he or she originally thought. As a result, job descriptions are usually rewritten. See chapter 4.

**Drill downs:** To dive into the Internet when looking for information needed to assist in finding recruiting information. See chapter 6.

**Employee referral programs:** Special internal programs in which companies reward their employees for providing referred individuals for open positions within the company. See chapter 6.

**Flipping:** Flip searching allows you to find Internet Web pages that are linked to a certain web site. The concept is that the employees of a targeted company will have their resume linked to their employer's web site. See chapter 6.

**Hall talk:** Useful information about the company's products, services, operations, or past that is not written down but only available by people talking informally. See chapter 1.

**Hiring manager:** The person who will be the direct supervisor and will eventually manage the employee for the open position. See chapter 1.

**Hiring probability:** The chances (represented as a percentage) of hiring a candidate as you go through the hiring process. See chapter 10.

**Keyword searching:** Using unique words that would be found in resumes of candidates during the search. See chapter 6.

**Outplacement:** The process of assisting unemployed individuals in finding new positions through specialized consulting. This includes, but is not limited to, resume rewrites, career coaching, practice interviews, and assistance in finding appropriate companies. See chapter 6.

**Passive candidates:** Candidates who are not actively seeking employment and typically do not have resumes on the Internet. See chapter 2.

**Peeling:** Peeling is used back out of a web site location with an address that may be very long and you need to "peel back" until you get to another location you are looking for. See chapter 6.

**Pending requisitions:** Any requisition that has not been approved, but is pending approval. See chapter 3.

**Proactive recruiter:** The proactive recruiter seeks out applicants and drives every step of the process to its ultimate conclusion. They even look for people who are not actively looking for a job or have their resumes posted on the Internet or are sending out resumes. See chapter 2.

**Reactive recruiter:** The reactive recruiters only respond when resumes come to them. They usually do not drive the process; they just forward the resumes and wait for a response. The resume flows into the HR department and is redirected to the proper hiring manager who in turn reviews it and either contacts the candidate for an interview or passes on it. If the hiring manager is too busy, the resumes stack up and may or may not be read. The recruiter will not get involved again until the candidate is scheduled for an interview. See chapter 2.

**Reality Management:** A twelve-step management program that is used in conjunction with talent balancing in order to manage the company, retain key employees, increase sales, and grow the organization. See chapter 1.

**Recruiting metrics:** Measurements of staffing activity in order to determine effective strategies. See chapter 10.

**Resume avalanche:** The problem of large quantities of resumes arriving in a short period of time and not being able to handle them. See chapter 7.

**Retained search:** Recruiting service in which an outside firm is paid a flat fee for finding qualified candidates. Commonly used when searching for upper management or hard to find professionals. See chapter 6.

**Salary compression:** Salary compression occurs when the industry increases salaries and a company does not. A three or four percent increase per year for the company's annual increase may be less that what the industry has been increasing. See chapter 2.

**Salary sticker shock:** When the employer finds out that the industry is now paying much more for their position than they are paying. See chapter 5.

**Sourcing:** The process of using candidates as a source of additional recruiting activity. See chapter 6.

**Staffing measurements:** Methods used to measure cost-to-hire, such as total hours worked, average hours per invoice, average hours per week, total staff hired, total increase in salary overhead, cost-to-hire percentage, number of hours per hire, time to staff, turnover, and/or any other statistics used for staffing. See chapter 6.

**Talent balancing:** The ability to balance the workload with the appropriate and competent staff. The objective is to be able to produce goods and services to meet corporate goals with a minimum number of employees at the highest level of productivity. At the same time, employees need to be challenged, comfortable with their responsibilities, and capable of meeting their goals. Talent balancing is a dynamic process—it always involves a specialized methodology in recruiting staff with an eye toward balancing current and future capacity and goals. It also builds teams that stay together and continue to be very efficient and productive. Finally, talent balancing includes an effective management technique in order to keep the staff challenged and fulfilled. See chapter 1.

**Temp to perm:** Also known as "try before you buy." Hiring an applicant on a temporary basis for a set time frame in order to see if he or she can do the work. If the work is acceptable, the person will be hired on a permanent or full-time basis. See chapter 1.

**X-raying:**   Finding all pages that are attached to a particular web site. Searching Internet pages inside a web site. Especially useful for searching universities and other organizations that might have resumes posted on site. See chapter 1.

# Index

## ABOUT THE AUTHOR

JIM STEDT is founder and president of Hartley & Associates, a Southern California–based staffing, management, and recruitment consulting firm. Since 1984 he has advised both startups and established firms in all areas of staffing and related human resource issues. Previously, he held a variety of management positions in several high-tech companies, including Varian Associates, GTE, and Microdata. He has written a monthly column on technology careers for *MicroTimes* magazine and has published a computer textbook, *Re-Organize*. He is the former president of Human Resources Independent Consultants Association and speaks to industry groups, colleges, and at networking workshops on hiring and job searching strategies.